P9-BYM-749

# CONTENTS

STUDY GUIDE

# PHILIP YANCEY

## WITH BRENDA QUINN

# THE JESUS I NEVER KNEW

ZONDERVAN®

GRAND RAPIDS, MICHIGAN 49530 USA

ZONDERVAN.COM/
AUTHORTRACKER

**Resources by Philip Yancey**

*The Jesus I Never Knew*
*What's So Amazing About Grace?*
*The Bible Jesus Read*
*Reaching for the Invisible God*
*Where Is God When It Hurts?*
*Disappointment with God*
*The Student Bible, General Edition* (with Tim Stafford)
*Meet the Bible* (with Brenda Quinn)
*Church: Why Bother?*
*Finding God in Unexpected Places*
*I Was Just Wondering*
*Soul Survivor*
*Rumors of Another World*
*Prayer*

**Books by Philip Yancey and Dr. Paul Brand**

*Fearfully and Wonderfully Made*
*In His Image*
*The Gift of Pain*
*In the Likeness of God*

**ZONDERVAN®**

*The Jesus I Never Knew, Study Guide*
Copyright © 1997 by Philip D. Yancey

Requests for information should be addressed to:

Zondervan, *Grand Rapids, Michigan 49530*

ISBN-10: 0-310-21805-5
ISBN-13: 978-0-310-21805-0

*Printed in the United States of America*

07 08 09 10 11 12 • 37 36 35 34 33 32 31 30 29 28 27 26 25

# USING THIS STUDY GUIDE

My study of Jesus began with a class I taught at LaSalle Street Church in Chicago. The use of movies about the life of Jesus, the stimulating discussion from class members, and my personal study all combined to give me a new view of Jesus—hence the title of my book *The Jesus I Never Knew.*

Yet all along I have had another goal in mind: I hope that my quest for Jesus serves as a guide for your own. In the end, what does it matter if a reader learns about "The Jesus Philip Yancey Never Knew"? What matters infinitely more is for *you* to get to know Jesus. If something I write can encourage that process, I am grateful.

For this reason, we have now produced a guide to help you delve into the topic on your own, either individually or in groups. I have been pleased to learn that people in small groups, meeting in churches and in homes, have been studying my book together. In fact, three people have sent me homemade study guides developed in these groups, and many more readers have written and asked for tools to help with their individual study of the book. (I thank Dick Malone especially for his unflagging support of this project.)

If you use this study guide by yourself, you should find that the questions build a bridge between my encounters with Jesus and your own. You may want to buy a blank notebook or personal journal (many bookstores sell these) in which to record your responses. Use this guide not as a textbook, feeling obligated to consider every question and fill in every blank, but rather as a series of suggestions.

Linger over questions that arouse something inside you. Skip questions that don't seem to speak to your heart, and ignore those activities we've included that are designed for a group. You may find that adding just one person to your study—a spouse or a close friend, perhaps—makes it much more meaningful.

Most of you, I imagine, will be using this study guide within a group. I like that notion. Jesus no longer lives in Nazareth or in Jerusalem; rather, he lives all over the world in a new form, the congregation of his followers described in the New Testament as the body of Christ. We are the ones whom God has called to represent his presence in the world, and I think it not only appropriate but essential that we meet together to consider exactly what form we should take. How can we be more like Jesus? How can we best embody him in the world?

The experts I most respect on group interactions are the folks who produce the Serendipity House products, including *The Serendipity Bible*. For several decades they have been leading small groups and training other leaders, and so I am thrilled to have one of their former employees, Brenda Quinn, working with me on this study guide. In a way I could never have done on my own, Brenda has taken my personal spiritual journey and adapted it into a form that others can use for their own journeys.

### *Advice for Small Groups*

Ideally, a small group should not exceed twelve or at most fifteen members. With anything larger than that, you'll likely find yourself reverting to a teacher-student structure in which the group leader dominates the discussion. In each session, as you'll see, we encourage you to break into even smaller groups of four to six. Sometimes the best sharing takes place in these smaller groups, which some people find less intimidating.

We recommend choosing a leader in advance of each week's meeting (it need not be the same leader every week). This study guide recommends certain group activities, and each session includes far more content than most groups can cover in a single session. A good leader can scout these questions and activities in advance, deciding which seem most pertinent to the needs of your group. The more willing the leader is to open up and share from his or her life, the more willing the group will be, so if you are the leader, take the role seriously. Think and pray about the group throughout the week before each meeting.

The study guide works best, of course, if everyone in the group has read the book we're studying, *The Jesus I Never Knew.* We follow its content chapter by chapter. Readers will need to have the book handy to read the sections referred to in this guide. Yet we also realize that in a busy world some people, no matter how well intentioned, do not get around to reading material in advance. Others read it so far in advance that by the time the meeting rolls around, they can barely remember the content. For this reason, we begin each session with a highly condensed summary of the chapter to be discussed. Some groups may choose to read this summary aloud to set the tone for the discussion to follow.

### Using Movies About Jesus

A number of readers have written me and inquired about the movies I used in my class in Chicago. I had been teaching a Sunday school class for eight years when we finally got to the New Testament. We had begun with Genesis, and chapter by chapter had been inching our way through the Bible. "Crawl through the Bible," we called the class, in honor of the pace. By the time we arrived at the Gospels, I was tired of talking and the class was tired of listening. We needed a change of pace, and that's when a friend suggested using movies about the life of Jesus. I went on a frenzied search for every video I could find, and the class began using the movies as a springboard for discussion.

We found Hollywood movies to be a wonderful addition to our study of Jesus. Here is how I used them: The week we studied the Temptation, for example, I would preview from my shelf of movies all the scenes that portrayed Jesus' temptation in the wilderness. I would select about five of the best, making sure they were three- to five-minute clips at the longest. When the class met, I would show these scenes on a big-screen television, starting with the corny and funny ones and progressing to the most evocative and profound.

While the movies were showing, I could watch their effect on the faces of the class members. Some scenes would draw out looks of puzzlement or bewilderment. Others would have the class members shaking their heads and saying, "No way it happened like that." And others would prompt thoughtful nods and remarks like, "Yes, maybe that was how it happened. That makes sense."

Taken together, the movies served an important role. They helped strip away our preconceptions of what took place in the scenes the Gospels describe in sparse detail. They made Jesus seem more human, made him come alive. We could picture ourselves back in his day, standing on the edge of the crowd, watching him and making judgments. How would we have responded to this man? Would we have invited him over for dinner, as Zacchaeus did? Turned away in sadness, as the rich young ruler did? Betrayed him, as Judas and Peter did?

Obviously, some of the film interpretations had to be wrong—they blatantly contradicted each other—but which ones? What really happened? After reacting to the film clips, we turned to the Gospel accounts, and from there the discussion took off. We read the accounts with open minds and a fresh point of view.

Yes, the movies did all these things. But I warn you, using movies in this way requires a lot of work! A leader must somehow accumulate a library of movies or find sources from which to rent or borrow them, then preview them each week and deal with the technological hurdles of presenting them effectively in a group setting.

To complicate matters, there are daunting copyright issues for those who show the movies to an organized group in a church building. (Showing movies in a home, with no admission charge, is OK.) The Motion Picture Licensing Corporation offers a renewable overall license for $95 per congregation, allowing you to show portions of movies at one location only for a year. Showing a video without the copyright owner's authorization is a copyright infringement and risks fines ranging from $500 to $20,000. For more details or to receive a license application, write the Motion Picture Licensing Corporation at P.O. Box 66970, Los Angeles, CA 90066 or call 800-462-8855 or 310-822-8855.

If somehow you can overcome all these hurdles, you may find that movies add a lot to your study of Jesus. At the back of this guide, in a section called "Movie Appendix," I have included a brief summary of the movies that may prove useful, along with my own very subjective evaluation. You'll also see that in this study guide, I list some portions of the movies that may apply to each week's meeting. I will give an approximate time frame for where in the movie each scene appears, but these are merely estimates; different editions of movies vary slightly in the timing of these scenes. When I say "forty-five-minute mark," you may find that the scene I refer to appears at the forty- or fifty-minute mark in your version. You'll have to scan forward or backward to find the precise place.

If you choose not to show movies each week during the study, you may want to consider holding a video night or two and selecting just a few of these movies to view together.

### Leading Group Discussion

Although group study is highly valuable, it carries challenges. You'll find that the challenges of group study mirror those experienced in the church, on a smaller and sometimes more intense scale. But don't let these challenges keep you from the bonding and growth achieved through life together. Enter with realistic expectations, knowing that, as in all relationships, there will be irritations and times when you don't feel like being together. You may face people you don't particularly like and probably even a period of disillusionment with the group. This is normal, just as it is normal in every family and in every friendship. Press on together. Most often you will find that God will bless individuals and group relationships in deep and lasting ways that far outweigh the difficult times you encounter.

As you meet together, keep the discussion moving. Don't be afraid of short silences, especially at first, when members are moving deeper into a topic. But don't let the discussion die. During a pause you may ask, "Does anyone have thoughts on this issue?" If silence continues or discussion remains minimal, don't be afraid to admit it: "Why don't we feel like talking about this today?"

The discussion may be less than provocative in other ways. It may start to snowball, with everyone agreeing with each other. In such cases you may need to play "devil's advocate" and argue the other side to force people to really think. At other times a few vocal people may dominate the discussion. You can counteract this by calling on others who have something to say, by watching especially for timid ones who are afraid to jump in, and even by taking the talkative one(s) aside after the meeting and asking them to share the time a little better.

Here are some suggestions for communicating throughout the discussion:

- When you believe that the speaker is making assumptions: "Why do you believe that? What have you experienced that makes you think so?"
- When you feel yourself becoming angry or uncomfortable: "Is anyone else feeling uneasy about this?" Don't feel a need

for all to come to agreement, but don't feel either that you should remain silent when you disagree with a statement. Further discussion will air feelings and prevent hidden emotions from erupting later in more destructive ways.

- When the main focus has been lost or an interesting point has been dropped amid further discussion: "Let's go back to the original question" or "Could we go back to what was said earlier about _____?" or "Could we talk a little more about _____?"
- When you sense the need to clarify: "Do you mean that Jesus didn't really rise from the dead or just that his resurrection was spiritual as well as physical?"
- When you sense there is more to what someone is saying: "Do you know why you feel this way? When did you first begin to feel this way?"
- When someone is obviously passionate about a viewpoint: Affirm their right to feel strongly and that they've been understood, by summarizing what they've said before agreeing or disagreeing—"You really feel strongly about this. You're saying that . . ."
- When someone is sharing something difficult and personal: "I've felt that way, too; I can understand" or "I haven't experienced that, so I appreciate your helping me to understand better what it was like."

Lastly—this probably goes without saying—be sensitive and respectful. Realize that some issues discussed in this study will be difficult. They may challenge long-held assumptions and practices. Remember that it takes time to process new ideas, especially those related to the Bible, our way of life, and our relationship with God. Much thought will continue after a group discussion, so don't feel a need to find all the answers in an hour or two. Most of us will continue thinking about these issues for the rest of our lives.

### *A Final Word*

I encourage you not to feel hemmed in by the structure we've set out in this study guide. We've divided the content into fourteen sessions, following the number of chapters in the book. Churches who follow a twelve- or thirteen-week cycle of study will need to make some adjustments. And if your group gets excited about the content of one session, by all means don't squelch the interest and slavishly turn to a new topic the next week. Follow up on the discussion. Each session provides guidelines as to how much time to spend in each section, assuming that you will be spending an hour meeting together. If you don't use films or if you meet for longer than an hour, adjust your time frame accordingly.

The same principle applies to individual questions. Don't cut off a stimulating discussion out of some obligation to plow through every single question. Likewise, if your group bogs down, move on until you find something that seems to generate interest. Remember, this small group study is not a school assignment with a goal of finishing all the material. You can certainly return to unfinished questions at home to work through them on your own, but don't feel an obligation to complete everything. Our goal is for you to encounter Jesus, and that may happen in unpredictable, unplanned ways. Allow room for God's Spirit to work in your group.

And by all means, have fun! You are embarking on a study of the most important individual who ever lived. Whatever else a person may think about him, Jesus most certainly was not boring.

# THE JESUS
# I THOUGHT I KNEW

———⬦⬦⬦———

I first got acquainted with Jesus when I was a child, singing "Jesus Loves Me" in Sunday school, addressing bedtime prayers to "Dear Lord Jesus," watching Bible club teachers move cutout figures across a flannelgraph board. I associated Jesus with Kool-Aid and sugar cookies and gold stars for good attendance.

Later, while attending a Bible college, I encountered a different image. A painting popular in those days depicted Jesus, hands outstretched, suspended in a Dalí-like pose over the United Nations building in New York City. In 1971 the film *The Gospel According to St. Matthew,* by Italian filmmaker Pier Paolo Pasolini, again helped to force a disturbing revaluation of my image of Jesus. In Pasolini's portrayal, in physical appearance Jesus favored those who would have been kicked out of Bible college and rejected by most churches. Among his contemporaries, the Bible says he somehow gained a reputation as a "winebibber and a glutton." Those in authority, whether religious or political, regarded him as a troublemaker, a disturber of the peace.

I have studied Jesus extensively in Catholic, liberal Protestant, and conservative evangelical seminaries. For two years I taught a class on the life of Jesus, using a variety of movies about his life as a springboard for discussion. In all of my study, I learned that whenever I returned to the Gospels, the fog that accompanied an academic approach seemed to lift. The films about Jesus helped restore Jesus' humanity. Jesus, I found, was far less tame than the Jesus I had met in Sunday school and Bible college. He seemed more emotional than the average person, not less. More passionate, not less. How is it, then, that the church has tamed such a character?

I have not written a book about Jesus because he is a great man who changed history. I am drawn to Jesus, irresistibly, because he positioned himself as the dividing point of life—my life. He said, "I tell you, whoever acknowledges me before men, the Son of Man will also acknowledge him before the angels of God" (Luke 12:8). According to Jesus, what I think about him and how I respond will determine my destiny for all eternity. Can I resolve my own inner tension between doubter and lover?

### *Viewing Jesus on Film,* OPTIONAL, 10 MINUTES

Note: In the introduction to this guide, you will find information about how to use movies as a study aid in your weekly groups or classes. In addition, in the back of this guide I have included a section titled "Movie Appendix," which lists some of the movies I've used for my teaching purposes, summarized in order of their potential usefulness.

Consider using clips from the following films as an opening to your time together.

> *Oh, God!:* At the twenty-five-minute mark, God, played by George Burns, answers some of the most troubling questions about him, with surprising answers.

> *Godspell:* Begins with a buoyant "Prepare ye the way of the Lord" scene.

> *Jesus of Nazareth,* tape 3: Jesus blasts the Pharisees, at the fifteen-minute mark. Also, five minutes after this scene, a member of the Sanhedrin debates who Jesus really is.

*Heaven:* See the segment "What Is God Like?" around the thirty-minute mark, but be sure to avoid the profanity. Also see a depiction of how Christians come across in the debate on "Can You Prove There's a Heaven?" around the fifty-three-minute mark.

*Jesus of Montreal:* Confused, modern actor on quest for Jesus, at the ten-minute mark.

*King of Kings I:* Classic portrayal of "Jesus meek and mild" healing a little girl's Roman soldier doll (!) at the thirty-five-minute mark.

## Seeing Jesus through Scripture

Read together the following passage:

Mark 6:1–6

## Looking at Jesus Within and Without, 25 MINUTES

You may be studying in a small group (less than twelve people) or in a larger group. For this section, break into groups of four to six people. Introduce yourselves to one another and tell about your family. How many siblings do you have? Where did you grow up? Are you married? Do you have children?

1. What did the people in Jesus' hometown think of him?

Imagine your brother or cousin or friend suddenly beginning to teach, with no formal training, in the city's biggest church. Imagine this person performing miracles. What would you think? What would people say?

2. Have you had someone close to you who really didn't know or understand you? How did this make you feel? Share as you feel comfortable. Do you think Jesus felt something similar?

3. How did the lack of understanding by Jesus' own people affect his use of his power through miracles?

   My friend isn't attending church, because she says Christians give Jesus a bad name. She claims the church could be the most powerful movement in the world if Christians would really get to know Jesus. What do you think of her opinion of Christians?

4. Do you think people today have any clearer picture of who Jesus is than did the people in his day? How do you think Jesus feels about the confusing portrait presented in today's church or by some individuals?

5. *The vision of Christ that thou dost see*
   *Is my vision's greatest enemy:*
   *Thine has a great hook nose like to mine....*
   *Both read the Bible day and night,*
   *But thou read'st black where I read white.*
   WILLIAM BLAKE

   In your mind's eye, what did Jesus look like? Tall? Short? Handsome? Curly hair or straight? Dark- or light-complected? Where did you get this picture of him (films, paintings, books, Sunday school)? Can you describe specific images from the past?

6. I mention several images of Jesus from my past. Which of these do you identify with?
   - A Victorian nanny who pats the heads of children and advises kindness to mummy and daddy
   - An ever friendly Mister Rogers—kind, gentle, and soft-spoken
   - A *Star Trek* Vulcan—calm, cool, and collected among excitable human beings on spaceship earth
   - A cosmic Christ hovering over the United Nations building
   - A radical hippie concerned with politics and peacemaking
   - A televangelist type—always spiritual, full of God-talk, and eager to prove his identity through miracles
   - Other:

Who or what prompted this vision? Talk about the church or religious environment in which you grew up. Has your vision of Jesus changed much?

7. What scares you about coming to know the real Jesus?

8. With the help of Jesus and this group, what do you most want to understand about Jesus?

Do you have any prayer needs to share with the group?

No one who meets Jesus ever stays the same.

### *Being Seen by Jesus,* 5–10 MINUTES

This last section of each study will give you a few minutes to personally invite Jesus into your study. It will be a time of silence, giving you a chance to share with him your questions, your needs, your thanks. You may not be accustomed to sharing quiet time together, but give it a try. This is a time to sit in the presence of Jesus as a corporate body and receive from him in a personal way. As you become comfortable, you'll find it a rich experience. Spend the time today in quiet, individual prayer. Feel free to add to the following prayer in the space provided. You may choose to keep a journal throughout the study. Bring it to class and use it during this time, to write your prayers, record your thoughts, or make notes on the discussion.

> *Dear Jesus, I am setting out on a journey that will bring me to a place of clearer vision, a place where I can better see you. A part of me wants only to close my eyes and stay where I am. But a part of me needs to know you better, needs to gaze on nothing but you. Enter the eyes of my mind, my heart. Help me along....*

## Further Glimpses of Jesus

- Look for art in your home that portrays Jesus. Bring some to class next week, including wall hangings, necklaces, pocket cards, and pictures in books.
- Look for old Christmas cards. Bring what you find to class next week.

## Gazing on Jesus This Week, OPTIONAL

You can integrate this study into your life throughout the week by using the following Scripture passages and book excerpt in your quiet moments. Reflect on these readings as your time allows.

Day 1: Isaiah 8:13–15; 9:1–7
Day 2: Matthew 1:18–2:23
Day 3: Mark 10:13–16; Luke 13:10–17
Day 4: Luke 11:37–54
Day 5: Luke 15:1–7

The people who hanged Christ never, to do them justice, accused Him of being a bore—on the contrary; they thought Him too dynamic to be safe. It has been left for later generations to muffle up that shattering personality and surround Him with an atmosphere of tedium. We have very efficiently pared the claws of the Lion of Judah, certified Him "meek and mild," and recommended Him as a fitting household pet for pale curates and pious old ladies. To those who knew Him, however, He in no way suggested a milk-and-water person; *they* objected to Him as a dangerous firebrand. True, He was tender to the unfortunate, patient with honest inquirers, and humble before Heaven; but He insulted respectable clergymen by calling them hypocrites; He referred to King Herod as "that fox"; He went to parties in disreputable company and was looked upon as a "gluttonous man and a winebibber, a friend of publicans and sinners"; He assaulted indignant tradesmen and threw them and their belongings out of the Temple; He drove a coach-and-horses through a number of sacrosanct and hoary regulations; He cured diseases by any means that came handy, with a shocking casualness in the matter of other people's pigs and property; He showed no proper deference for wealth or social position; when confronted with neat dialectical traps, He displayed a paradoxical humour that affronted serious-minded people, and He retorted by asking disagreeably searching questions that could not be answered by rule of thumb. He was emphatically not a dull man in His human lifetime, and if He was God, there can be nothing dull about God either. But He had "a daily beauty in His life that made us ugly," and officialdom felt that the established order of things would be more secure without Him. So they did away with God in the name of peace and quietness.*

---

*Dorothy L. Sayers, *Christian Letters to a Post-Christian World* (Grand Rapids, Eerdmans, 1969), 15–16.

# BIRTH:
# THE VISITED PLANET

———— ⚌⚌ ————

Sorting through a stack of Christmas cards, I notice that all kinds of symbols and sentiments have edged their way into the Christmas celebration. But when I compare today's Christmas cards to the Gospel accounts of the first Christmas, I hear a very different tone. In the Gospels, I sense mainly disruption at work. Mary was a pregnant teenager and a virgin! The news an angel brought couldn't have been entirely welcome to Mary or Joseph, considering the closely knit Jewish community in which they lived. In contrast to what the cards would have us believe, Christmas did not sentimentally simplify life on planet earth.

The facts of Christmas, rhymed in carols, recited by children in church plays, illustrated on cards, have become so familiar that it is easy to miss the message behind the facts. We observe a mellow, domesticated holiday purged of any hint of scandal. Above all, we purge from it any reminder of how the story that began at Bethlehem turned out at Calvary. After reading the birth stories once more, I ask myself, *If Jesus came to reveal God to us, then what do I learn about God from that first Christmas?*

*Viewing Jesus on Film,* OPTIONAL, 10 MINUTES

Consider using clips from the following films as an opening to your time together. Display any artwork or Christmas cards that group members have brought.

Note: Two movies, *Nativity* and *A Child Called Jesus,* are sometimes shown on television around Christmas, but I know of no copies commercially available. The latter is based largely on the Apocryphal Gospels.

> *The Greatest Story Ever Told,* tape 1: Effective portrayal of Jesus' family's exile in Egypt, around the twenty-minute mark.

> *Cotton Patch Gospel:* One of the few film portrayals of Jesus in childhood (getting lost in the temple), at the fourteen-minute mark.

> *Jesus of Nazareth,* tape 1: Detailed depictions of all the birth stories, in the first hour of the tape.

> *King of Kings II,* tape 1: Wise men, slaughter of the infants, and return to Nazareth, beginning around the fifteen-minute mark.

> *The Gospel According to St. Matthew:* Flight into Egypt, slaughter of the innocents, beginning at the fourteen-minute mark.

*Seeing Jesus through Scripture,* 15 MINUTES

Read one or both of the following Scripture passages:

Matthew 1:18–25
Luke 2:1–20

Now read together the following story by J. B. Phillips. You may want to select a narrator, a little angel, and a senior angel to read the parts.

### *The Visited Planet*

Once upon a time a very young angel was being shown round the splendour and glories of the universes by a senior and experienced angel. To tell the truth, the little angel was beginning to be tired and a little bored. He had been shown whirling galaxies and blazing suns, infinite distances in the deathly cold of inter-stellar space, and to his mind there seemed to be an awful lot of it all. Finally he was shown the galaxy of which our planetary system is but a small part. As the two of them drew near to the star which we call our sun and to its circling planets, the senior angel pointed to a small and rather insignificant sphere turning very slowly on its axis. It looked as dull as a dirty tennis-ball to the little angel, whose mind was filled with the size and glory of what he had seen.

"I want you to watch that one particularly," said the senior angel, pointing with his finger.

"Well, it looks very small and rather dirty to me," said the little angel. "What's special about that one?"

"That," replied his senior solemnly, "is the Visited Planet."

"Visited?" said the little one. "You don't mean visited by—?"

"Indeed I do. That ball, which I have no doubt looks to you small and insignificant and not perhaps overclean, has been visited by our young Prince of Glory." And at these words he bowed his head reverently.

"But how?" queried the younger one. "Do you mean that our great and glorious Prince, with all these wonders and splendours of His Creation, and millions more that I'm sure I haven't seen yet, went down in Person to this fifth-rate little ball? Why should He do a thing like that?"

"It isn't for us," said his senior a little stiffly, "to question His 'why's,' except that I must point out to you that He is not impressed by size and numbers, as you seem to

23

be. But that He really went I know, and all of us in Heaven who know anything know that. As to why He became one of them—how else do you suppose could He visit them?"

The little angel's face wrinkled in disgust.

"Do you mean to tell me," he said, "that He stooped so low as to become one of those creeping, crawling creatures of that floating ball?"

"I do, and I don't think He would like you to call them 'creeping, crawling creatures' in that tone of voice. For, strange as it may seem to us, He loves them. He went down to visit them to lift them up to become like Him."

The little angel looked blank. Such a thought was almost beyond his comprehension.

"Close your eyes for a moment," said the senior angel, "and we will go back in what they call Time."

While the little angel's eyes were closed and the two of them moved nearer to the spinning ball, it stopped its spinning, spun backwards quite fast for a while, and then slowly resumed its usual rotation.

"Now look!" And as the little angel did as he was told, there appeared here and there on the dull surface of the globe little flashes of light, some merely momentary and some persisting for quite a time.

"Well, what am I seeing now?" queried the little angel.

"You are watching this little world as it was some thousands of years ago," returned his companion. "Every flash and glow of light that you see is something of the Father's knowledge and wisdom breaking into the minds and hearts of people who live upon the earth. Not many people, you see, can hear His Voice or understand what He says, even though He is speaking gently and quietly to them all the time."

"Why are they so blind and deaf and stupid?" asked the junior angel rather crossly.

"It is not for us to judge them. We who live in the Splendour have no idea what it is like to live in the dark.

We hear the music and the Voice like the sound of many waters every day of our lives, but to them—well, there is much darkness and much noise and much distraction upon the earth. Only a few who are quiet and humble and wise hear His voice. But watch, for in a moment you will see something truly wonderful."

The earth went on turning and circling round the sun, and then quite suddenly, in the upper half of the globe, there appeared a light, tiny but so bright in its intensity that both the angels hid their eyes.

"I think I can guess," said the little angel in a low voice. "That was the Visit, wasn't it?"

"Yes, that was the Visit. The Light Himself went down there and lived among them; but in a moment, and you will be able to tell that even with your eyes closed, the light will go out."

"But why? Could He not bear their darkness and stupidity? Did He have to return here?"

"No, it wasn't that," returned the senior angel. His voice was stern and sad. "They failed to recognise Him for Who He was—or at least only a handful knew Him. For the most part they preferred their darkness to His Light, and in the end they killed Him."

"The fools, the crazy fools! They don't deserve —"

"Neither you nor I, nor any other angel, knows why they were so foolish and so wicked. Nor can we say what they deserve or don't deserve. But the fact remains, they killed our Prince of Glory while He was Man amongst them."

"And that I suppose was the end? I see the whole Earth has gone black and dark. All right, I won't judge them, but surely that is all they could expect?"

"Wait, we are still far from the end of the story of the Visited Planet. Watch now, but be ready to cover your eyes again."

In utter blackness the earth turned round three times, and then there blazed with unbearable radiance a point of light.

"What now?" asked the little angel, shielding his eyes.

"They killed Him all right, but He conquered death. The thing most of them dread and fear all their lives He broke and conquered. He rose again, and a few of them saw Him and from then on became His utterly devoted slaves."

"Thank God for that," said the little angel.

"Amen. Open your eyes now, the dazzling light has gone. The Prince has returned to His Home of Light. But watch the Earth now."

As they looked, in place of the dazzling light there was a bright glow which throbbed and pulsated. And then as the Earth turned many times little points of light spread out. A few flickered and died; but for the most part the lights burned steadily, and as they continued to watch, in many parts of the globe there was a glow over many areas.

"You see what is happening?" asked the senior angel. "The bright glow is the company of loyal men and women He left behind, and with His help they spread the glow and now lights begin to shine all over the Earth."

"Yes, yes," said the little angel impatiently, "but how does it end? Will the little lights join up with each other? Will it all be light, as it is in Heaven?"

His senior shook his head. "We simply do not know," he replied. "It is in the Father's hands. Sometimes it is agony to watch and sometimes it is joy unspeakable. The end is not yet. But now I am sure you can see why this little ball is so important. He has visited it; He is working out His Plan upon it."

"Yes, I see, though I don't understand. I shall never forget that this is the Visited Planet."*

---

*J. B. Phillips, *New Testament Christianity* (London: Hodder & Stoughton, 1962), 27–33.

### *Looking at Jesus Within and Without,* 20 MINUTES

If you are in a larger group, break into groups of four to six people. Introduce yourselves and briefly tell what you did for Christmas last year.

1. Share any artwork or Christmas cards that group members have brought to class, if you have not already done so. Even if your group has no Christmas cards, try to answer these questions: What kinds of scenes do today's Christmas cards display? What emotions and real-life circumstances do these Christmas cards fail to portray?

2. Think about the circumstances Mary and Joseph were in during the time of Jesus' birth. Has anyone in your group had similar experiences?
   - Parents' disapproval of a wedding
   - An unplanned pregnancy
   - An unusual labor experience
   - Caring for a newborn without the help of friends or extended family

3. Who did Mary and Joseph have to turn to for support during these early days and years? Who do you turn to for support in times of crisis?

4. What do you imagine Jesus was like as a baby? Did he cry? Get hurt? Make mistakes in grammar as he learned language?

27

5. If Jesus came to reveal God to us, what do we learn about God from that first Christmas? Write down the first words that come to mind.

   I have set down some of my own words. Do you agree with them?

   • What especially strikes you about God as *humble* (pp. 36–37)?

   • In most religious traditions, *fear* is the primary emotion when one approaches God. What about the Christmas story makes God *approachable* (pp. 37–39)?

   Read the middle three paragraphs on page 40, beginning with the words, "Perhaps the best way . . ." Which of these facts about Jesus surprise you? How do they differ from normal depictions of Jesus? How do they make you feel toward him?

6. What has Christmas meant to you in the past? What would you like it to mean?

Do you have any prayer needs you would like to share with the group?

## *Being Seen by Jesus,* 5–10 Minutes

Spend this time in quiet, individual prayer and meditation. You may want to reflect on Mary's Song, the Magnificat, in Luke 1:46–55. If you choose to write a prayer, you can use the space provided or use your journal. You can also choose to write notes or reactions to today's study. This is a time to quiet yourself and reflect on Jesus. He may use this time to speak to you.

> *O here and now our endless journey stops.*
> *O here and now our endless journey starts.*
>
> W. H. AUDEN

## *Further Glimpses of Jesus*

- Plan to visit a museum that exhibits art depicting Jesus. Study the physical representations of Jesus, the moods the pieces evoke, and the emotions the characters display.
- During Easter we can attend a Passion play to remember anew the events of Jesus' crucifixion and resurrection. Think in the coming week about your typical celebration of Christmas. How much of it involves reflection on Jesus' birth? What do you do, or could you do, to remember Jesus' birth as it really was, rather than as it is depicted in its sentimentalized form?

## *Gazing on Jesus This Week,* Optional

You can integrate this study into your life throughout the week by using in your quiet moments the Scripture passages, and the excerpt from *The Jesus I Never Knew,* that follow. Reflect on these readings as your time allows.

Day 1: Luke 2:21–40
Day 2: Matthew 3:1–12
Day 3: Luke 2:41–52
Day 4: Matthew 3:13–17
Day 5: John 1:1–18

Excerpt: Read again the five paragraphs on pages 41–42 beginning with the heading, "Courageous. In 1993 ..."

# BACKGROUND:
# JEWISH ROOTS AND SOIL

⸻ ∞ ⸻

As a boy growing up in a WASP community in Atlanta, Georgia, I did not know a single Jew. Not until my early twenties did I befriend a Jewish photographer who disabused me of many notions about his race. He described what it was like to lose twenty-seven members of his family to the Holocaust. He acquainted me with Elie Wiesel, Chaim Potok, Martin Buber, and other Jewish writers, and after these encounters I began reading the New Testament through new eyes. How could I have missed it! Jesus' true-blue Jewishness leaps out from Matthew's very first sentence, which introduces him as "the son of David, the son of Abraham."

Martin Buber said, "We Jews know [Jesus] in a way—in the impulses and emotions of his essential Jewishness—that remains inaccessible to the Gentiles subject to him." Those of us who are Gentiles face the constant danger of letting Jesus' Jewishness, and even his humanity, slip away. In historical fact, we are the ones who have co-opted *their* Jesus. I can no more understand Jesus apart from his Jewishness than I can understand Gandhi apart from his Indianness. I need to go back, way back, and picture Jesus as a first-century Jew with a phylactery on his wrist and Palestinian dust on his sandals.

I learned many things as I examined more closely the fact that Jesus was a Jew:

- For Jews who considered the name Jesus common, like "Bob" or "Joe" today, and who did not pronounce the Honorable Name of God, the idea that an ordinary person with a name like Jesus could be the Son of God seemed utterly scandalous.
- Within a generation after Jesus lived, Roman soldiers razed Jerusalem. The young Christian church accepted the destruction of the temple as a sign of the end of the covenant between God and Israel, and after the first century very few Jews converted to Christianity. Christians appropriated Jewish Scriptures, renaming them "Old Testament," and put an end to most Jewish customs.
- Sepphoris was a gleaming city just three miles north of Nazareth. This city served as the capital of Galilee, second in importance only to Jerusalem. Not once, however, do the Gospels record that Jesus visited or even mentioned the city. He gave centers of wealth and political power a wide berth.
- At the time of Jesus' birth, Palestine was quiet under the iron thumb of Herod the Great. Years of long wars with Rome had drained both the spirit and the resources of the Jews.
- Jesus managed to confound and alienate each of the major groups in Palestine: Essenes, Zealots, the Sanhedrin, Sadducees, Pharisees. For all their differences, these groups shared one goal: to preserve what was distinctively Jewish, no matter what. To that goal, Jesus represented a threat. He held out another way, different from their choices of either separation or collaboration with Rome. His focus was on the kingdom of God.

As a member of a minority race, how would I have responded to oppression by the mighty Roman Empire? What kind of Jew would I have made in the first century? Would Jesus have won me over?

*Viewing Jesus on Film,* OPTIONAL, 10 MINUTES

Consider using clips from the following films as an opening to your time together.

> *Oh, God!:* At the eighty-minute mark, the movie deals with the issue of God coming as a busboy. What makes him so hard to believe? Why does God appear in such unpredictable forms?

> *The Greatest Story Ever Told,* tape 1: Portrayal of the scene in Luke 4, in which Jesus returns to his hometown, at the ninety-eight-minute mark.

> *The Last Temptation of Christ:* Jesus' return to Nazareth, at the seventy-five-minute mark.

> *King of Kings II,* tape 1: The movie opens with excellent historical background on Rome's invasion of Israel, and the appointment of Herod.

> *The Gospel According to St. Matthew:* Jesus' disputes with leading Jews, at the eighty-seven-minute mark.

> *Jesus:* Jesus visits his hometown and announces his identity, at the thirteen-minute mark.

### Seeing Jesus through Scripture

[Leader: Consider obtaining a cassette or CD titled *Shalom Jerusalem.* This music was performed live in Jerusalem. It should be available through your local Christian bookstore. Have this music playing at the beginning of the meeting. You may want to keep it playing softly throughout the meeting. It will help set the tone for today's focus on Jesus' Jewish roots.]

Following are the Scripture passages you will focus on in this study. Wait until you are instructed to read them later in the session.

Matthew 5:17–20
Matthew 5:21–26
Matthew 5:43–48
Matthew 6:1–4
Matthew 7:1–6

### *Looking at Jesus Within and Without,* 25 MINUTES

If you are in a larger group, break into groups of four to six people. Introduce yourselves if necessary and tell the group which holiday was your favorite as a child. Why was this one your favorite?

1. As a boy, I did not know a single Jew. I pictured Jews as foreigners with thick accents and strange hats who lived in Brooklyn or some such faraway place, where they all studied to become psychiatrists and musicians. I knew Jews had something to do with World War II, but I had heard little about the Holocaust.

   Did you grow up interacting with Jewish people? Explain. Do you have friends or acquaintances or any other contacts now with the Jewish culture? What have you come to appreciate about the Jewish culture?

   If you are Jewish, what has been your experience with people who are not Jewish? Have you ever felt prejudice from non-Jewish Christians? Even if you are not Jewish, have you ever been in a position in which you felt like a minority?

2. Jesus attended Jewish festivals, worshiped in the synagogue and temple, followed Jewish customs, and spoke in terms his fellow Jews would understand. How much do you know about the Jewish faith, Jewish customs, and Jewish holidays?

Test your knowledge. What do you know about the following Jewish holidays or terms? See the end of this session for answers.
• Phylactery
• Rosh Hashanah
• Yom Kippur
• Passover
• Passover Seder
• Haggadah
• Hanukkah

3. In an article in *Christianity Today* on racial reconciliation, Harold Myra says, "Integrity demands we try to understand the depth of others' experiences, especially those who have muddied their hands trying to alleviate nearly impossible situations."* Myra is encouraging readers to enter into the world of those in other racial and ethnic groups, to better understand their perspectives. Can you tell about a time when you attempted this?

---

*Harold Myra, "Racial Reconciliation Begins with You: Let's Break Down Barriers That Divide Us," *Christianity Today* (March 6, 1995), 19.

4. Is it possible to read the Gospels without blinders on? Jews read with suspicion, preparing to be scandalized. Christians read through the refracting lenses of church history. Both groups, I believe, would do well to pause and reflect on Matthew's first words: "A record of the genealogy of Jesus Christ the son of David, the son of Abraham." "The son of David" speaks of Jesus' messianic line, which Jews should not ignore; "a title which he would not deny to save his life cannot have been without significance for him," notes C. H. Dodd. "The son of Abraham" speaks of Jesus' Jewish line, which we Christians dare not ignore, either. Jaroslav Pelikan writes,

> Would there have been such anti-Semitism, would there have been so many pogroms [organized massacres], would there have been an Auschwitz, if every Christian church and every Christian home had focused its devotion on icons of Mary not only as mother of God and Queen of Heaven but as the Jewish maiden and the new Miriam, and on icons of Christ not only as a Pantocrator [leader, ruler] but as *Rabbi Jeshua bar-Joseph*, Rabbi Jesus of Nazareth?

In twentieth-century America, what blinders do Christians wear that may affect how they read the Gospels?

Do you think the Christian church could benefit from remembering Jewish holidays? How does your church and/or home actively remember Y'shua's Jewishness (*Y'shua* is Hebrew for *Jesus* and is the preferred spelling by many Hebrew [Jewish] Christians today)? If you don't incorporate the Jewish culture into your church or home, what ideas do you have on how this could be done?

5. As I read the Gospels, I try to project myself back into those times. How would I have responded to oppression? Would I have striven to be a model citizen and keep out of trouble, to live and let live? Would I have been tempted by fiery insurrectionists? Would I have fought back in more devious ways, by avoiding taxes perhaps? Or would I have thrown my energies into a religious movement and shunned political controversies? What kind of Jew would I have made in the first century?

Eight million Jews lived in the Roman Empire then, just over a quarter of them in Palestine itself. In many ways, the plight of the Jewish leaders resembled that of the Russian churches under Stalin. They could cooperate, which meant submitting to government interference, or they could go their own way, which meant harsh persecution. In response, Jews splintered into parties that followed different paths of collaboration or separatism (pp. 61–63):

- Essenes: pacifistic; withdrew into monkish communities in the desert; committed to purity through rules on cleanliness, diet, simplicity, and communal living.
- Zealots: advocated armed revolt to throw out impure foreigners; some were political terrorists, some were "morals police."

- The Sanhedrin: collaborationists who tried to work within the system; cooperated with Romans in scouting out any sign of insurrection. Caiphas was high priest of the Sanhedrin.
- Sadducees: the most blatant collaborationists; humanistic in theology—did not believe in an afterlife or divine intervention on this earth; enjoyed life with many material possessions.
- Pharisees: the popular party of the middle class; often on the fence, vacillating between separatism and collaboration; held to high standards of purity and treated Jews with lower standards "as Gentiles"; suffered their share of persecution; believed passionately in the Messiah; hesitated to follow too quickly after any impostor or miracle worker who might bring disaster on the nation; picked their battles carefully.

As Christians today respond to an increasingly secular society, do they adopt approaches similar to those of these groups? Can you think of leaders or groups today who resemble these groups of Jesus' day?

Which of the above groups do you have a tendency to resemble? Would Jesus have won you over?

6. Read the following Scripture passages and discuss how Jesus' words can speak to modern-day Christians who resemble the group next to each passage.

- Matthew 5:17–20 (Sadducees)
- Matthew 5:21–26 (Pharisees)
- Matthew 5:43–48 (Zealots)
- Matthew 6:1–4 (Essenes)
- Matthew 7:1–6 (Sanhedrin)

7. The Jews were, in effect, erecting a fence around their culture, in hopes of saving their tiny nation of high ideals from the pagans around them. Could God have liberated the Jews from Rome as he had once liberated them from Egypt?

The Jews were looking for a Messiah in the form of an earthly king, a powerful ruler. What kind of leader is our society looking for today? What are Christians looking for?

Do you have any prayer needs to share with the group?

## *Being Seen by Jesus*, 5-10 MINUTES

Spend this time in quiet, individual prayer, journaling, or note taking. Feel free to add on to the following prayer in the space provided.

> *Jesus, Y'shua, Messiah, I do not know you in all your fullness. My understanding is limited. You are foreign to me, and I want to protect my well-defined religious world. You are a*

*threat. You don't always make sense to me. Just when I feel I'm on the right track, you challenge me again. I feel frustrated, yet I can't shake your love for me. It's bigger than my frustration or my misunderstanding. You keep inviting me to come closer. I do want to know you more completely. Show me the way. . . .*

### *Further Glimpses of Jesus*

- Find out this week about the Jewish synagogues and Hebrew Christian congregations in your area. (Look in the phone book under *Synagogues* and *Churches—Jewish Christian*.) Make plans to visit one. Ask about their celebrations of Jewish holidays and plan to attend one of these services later.
- Visit the library and pick up a book by Elie Wiesel, Chaim Potok, Martin Buber, Letty Cottin Pogrebin *(Deborah, Golda, and Me: Being Female and Jewish in America)*, or any other Jewish writer. Learn from them about the Jewish culture.
- Consider ordering the books *Christ in the Passover* by Ceil and Moishe Rosen ($6.95) and *Celebrate Passover Haggadah: A Christian Presentation of the Traditional Jewish Festival* by Joan R. Lipis ($3.95). Write Purple Pomegranate Productions, 80 Page Street, San Francisco, CA 94102-5914 or call 415-864-3900.

### *Gazing on Jesus This Week,* Optional

Focus on the following Scripture passages this week during quiet moments as you reflect on the person of Jesus. Use these passages as your time allows.

Day 1: Matthew 1:1–17; Luke 3:21–38
Day 2: Luke 4:14–30
Day 3: Matthew 9:1–8
Day 4: Matthew 9:9–17
Day 5: Matthew 10:1–42

Answers:

- *Phylactery.* One of two small, square leather boxes containing slips inscribed with Scripture passages, traditionally worn on the left arm and forehead by Jewish men during weekday morning prayers.
- *Rosh Hashanah.* The Jewish New Year, a solemn occasion celebrated on the first, or first and second, of Tishri (usually late September or early October).
- *Yom Kippur.* The holiest Jewish holiday, celebrated on the tenth day of Tishri (usually late September or early October), on which fasting and prayer for the atonement of sins are prescribed. Also called "Day of Atonement." In the Old Testament, this was the one day each year when the high priest entered the Most Holy Place.
- *Passover.* A festival beginning on the evening of the fourteenth of Nisan, March or April, and traditionally celebrated for eight days. It commemorates the escape of the Jews from Egypt (Exodus 12).
- *Passover Seder.* The feast commemorating the exodus of the Israelites from Egypt, celebrated on the first evening, or first two evenings, of Passover. The Last Supper was a Passover meal. For Christians who have never taken part in a Seder meal, it is a fascinating celebration involving food that is symbolic of both the Jewish plight and deliverance from Egypt and humankind's plight and deliverance from sin. This traditional Jewish celebration, dating back centuries before Christ, remembers the bondage of Israel, commemorates the redemption from slavery, and looks toward the

Messiah as the ultimate Redeemer. Many Christians find it a truly joyous celebration to take part in this meal, identifying Christ as its Completor.

- *Haggadah.* The book containing the story of the Exodus and the ritual of the Seder, read at the Passover Seder.
- *Hanukkah (or Chanukah).* A Jewish festival beginning on the twenty-fifth day of the month of Kislev (sometime in December) and lasting eight days. It commemorates the victory of the Maccabees over the Syrians in 165 B.C. and the rededication of the temple at Jerusalem. Also called "Feast of Lights," "Feast of Dedication."

WEEK FOUR

# TEMPTATION:
# SHOWDOWN IN THE DESERT

---

Do we humans enjoy too much freedom? We have the freedom to harm and kill each other, to fight global wars, to despoil our planet. We are even free to defy God. Couldn't Jesus have devised some irrefutable proof to silence all skeptics, tilting the odds decisively in God's favor? As it is, God seems easy to ignore or deny.

Jesus' first "official" act as an adult, when he went into the wilderness to meet the accuser face-to-face, gave him the occasion to address these problems. Satan himself tempted the Son of God to change the rules and achieve his goals by a dazzling shortcut method. But more than Jesus' character was at stake on the sandy plains of Palestine; human history hung in the balance.

Satan tempted Jesus toward the good parts of being human without the bad: to savor the taste of bread without being subject to the fixed rules of hunger and of agriculture, to confront risk with no real danger, to enjoy fame and power without the prospect of painful rejection—in short, to wear a crown but not a cross.

Did Jesus not realize that people want more than anything else to worship what is established beyond dispute? As Fyodor Dostoevsky's Grand Inquisitor says in *The Brothers Karamazov,* "Instead of taking possession of men's freedom, you increased it, and burdened the spiritual kingdom of mankind with its sufferings forever. You desired man's free love, that he should follow you freely, enticed and taken captive by you." By resisting Satan's temptations to override human freedom, the Inquisitor maintains, Jesus made himself far too easy to reject. He surrendered his greatest advantage: the power to compel belief. Fortunately, continues the sly Inquisitor, the church recognized the error and corrected it, and has been relying on miracle, mystery, and authority ever since.

If I read history correctly, many others have yielded to the very temptation Jesus resisted: the Spanish Inquisition and the Protestant version in Geneva, Adolph Hitler, Jim Jones, David Koresh, and even today's manipulation enacted in churches by those with skills learned from politicians, salespeople, and advertising copywriters.

I am quick to diagnose these flaws, yet when I examine myself, I find that I too am vulnerable to the Temptation. Sometimes I wish God used a heavier touch. My faith suffers from too much freedom, too many temptations to disbelieve. At times I want God to overcome my doubts with certainty, to give final proofs of his existence and his concern. I also lack the willpower to resist shortcut solutions to human needs. I lack the patience to allow God to work in a slow, "gentlemanly" way. I want to compel others to help accomplish the causes I believe in. I am willing to trade away certain freedoms for the guarantee of safety and protection. I am willing to trade away even more for the chance to realize my ambitions.

When I feel these temptations rising within me, I return to the story of Jesus and Satan in the desert. Jesus' resistance against Satan's temptations preserved for me the very freedom I exercise when I face my own temptations. I pray for the same trust and patience that Jesus showed.

*Viewing Jesus on Film,* OPTIONAL, 10 MINUTES

Consider using clips from the following films as an opening to your time together.

*The Gospel Road:* Covers the Temptation, at about the six-minute mark.

*The Greatest Story Ever Told,* tape 1: See the temptation scene, at the thirty-three-minute mark.

*The Last Temptation of Christ:* With its title, you can expect this movie to put prime emphasis on the Temptation; at the fifty-four-minute mark.

*Cotton Patch Gospel:* Interesting rendition of the Temptation, at the twenty-seven-minute mark. Also, see the spoof of a TV evangelist, at the fifty-three-minute mark.

*Jesus of Montreal:* The temptation scenes are reintroduced into a modern context, at about the one-hour mark and also at the seventy-three-minute mark.

*King of Kings I:* Cecil B. DeMille repositions the timing of the Temptation to occur at the end of Jesus' life, around the fifty-minute mark.

*Jesus:* Straightforward depiction of the Temptation, at the eleven-minute mark.

### Seeing Jesus through Scripture

Read together the following passage:

Matthew 4:1–11

### Looking at Jesus Within and Without, 25 MINUTES

If you are in a larger group, break into groups of four to six. Introduce yourselves if necessary and tell the group which food is most tempting to you. If you were fasting in the desert, what food images would fill your mind?

1. If Jesus was all alone when it happened, how do you think the gospel writers learned about this encounter in the desert between Jesus and Satan? What does that say about

the importance of the story? Do you ever reveal your temptations to anyone else?

2. The British poet Gerard Manley Hopkins presents the Temptation as something of a get-acquainted session between Jesus and Satan. In Hopkins's view, Satan is in the dark about the Incarnation and does not know for certain whether Jesus is an ordinary man or a theophany (an appearance of God, a divine manifestation) or perhaps an angel with limited powers, like himself. Satan challenges Jesus to perform miracles as a means of scouting his adversary's powers.

Martin Luther goes further, speculating that throughout his life Jesus "conducted himself so humbly and associated with sinful men and women, and as a consequence was not held in great esteem," on account of which "the devil overlooked him and did not recognize him. For the devil is farsighted; he looks only for what is big and high and attaches himself to that; he does not look at that which is low down and beneath himself" (p. 71).

Did Satan know who Jesus was? How do Hopkins's and Luther's views on Satan in the story of the Temptation fit with your own views? What do you learn about Satan from this story?

3. As Malcolm Muggeridge sees it (see quote on pp. 72–73), the Temptation revolved around the question uppermost

in the minds of Jesus' countrymen: What should the Messiah look like?

- A people's Messiah, who could turn stones into bread to feed the multitudes?
- A Torah Messiah, standing tall at the lofty pinnacle of the temple?
- A king Messiah, ruling over not just Israel but all the kingdoms of earth?

What kind of Messiah are you looking to find? Do you want a God who will fix social problems and relieve the suffering in our world? Or a God who unites all the churches and clarifies the one right way? Or a God who brings worldwide peace? Or maybe you're more drawn to a God who will meet all your needs? Or a God who will guarantee your health and safety? Or a God who will cause others to respect and acclaim you? Is there anything wrong in having these hopes or expectations of God?

4. After traveling in the former Soviet Union and speaking with the people, I came away with the strong sense that we Christians would do well to relearn the basic lesson of the Temptation. Goodness cannot be imposed externally, from the top down; it must grow internally, from the bottom up.

Do you agree with this statement? Think of someone who has inspired you toward goodness—a parent, mentor, pastor, teacher, friend. What made them effective?

5. In the words of George McDonald (p. 77), Jesus "resisted every impulse to work more rapidly for a lower good."

   I want God to take a more active role in my personal history. I want quick and spectacular answers to my prayers, healing for my diseases, protection and safety for my loved ones. I want a God without ambiguity, one to whom I can point for the sake of my doubting friends.

   When I think these thoughts, I recognize in myself a thin, hollow echo of the challenge that Satan hurled at Jesus two thousand years ago. God resists those temptations now as Jesus resisted them on earth, settling instead for a slower, gentler way.

   Do you ever wish Jesus would "hurry up" his work in your life—for example, in your job, dating relationships, friendships, marriage, raising your children, volunteer work, success in your church? What makes you spiritually impatient? What do you do with that impatience? Are you tempted to compromise Jesus' way to achieve what might seem to you to be God's best?

6. The more I get to know Jesus, the more impressed I am with what Ivan Karamazov (in Dostoevsky's novel) called "the miracle of restraint." It is Jesus' refusal to perform and to overwhelm. As I survey the rest of Jesus' life, I see that the pattern of restraint established in the desert persisted throughout his life. I never sense Jesus twisting a person's arm. Rather, he stated the consequences of a choice, then threw the decision back to the other party. He had no

compulsion to convert the entire world in his lifetime or to cure people who were not ready to be cured.

How did Jesus enter your life? Did you feel pressure from him? From others?

How do you approach sharing Jesus with others? Do you inwardly feel a "savior complex," a compulsion to cure others' problems? Do you ever fall into the temptation to misrepresent yourself or manipulate in some way in order to "win souls"? Or do you fall into the opposite temptation and shy away from all evangelism?

Do you have any prayer needs you'd like to express to the group?

### *Being Seen by Jesus,* 5-10 MINUTES

Spend this time in quiet, individual prayer or meditation. If you choose to write a prayer, you may use the space provided or your journal. You can also use the time to make notes to yourself on today's study. You may want to reflect on Hebrews 4:14–16:

Therefore, since we have a great high priest who has gone through the heavens, Jesus the Son of God, let us hold firmly to the faith we profess. For we do not have a high priest who is unable to sympathize with our weaknesses, but we have one who has been tempted in every way, just as we are—yet was without sin. Let us then approach the throne of grace with confidence, so that we may receive mercy and find grace to help us in our time of need.

### *Further Glimpses of Jesus*

- This week make a list of three things in your life that are troubling you. For each, try to determine what is at the root of your feeling. Does it resemble any of the temptations Jesus faced? How does his response to Satan speak to your trouble?
- This week carry with you the words "miracle of restraint." Think about this characteristic of Jesus and pray that his miracle would become more real in your life.

### *Gazing on Jesus This Week,* OPTIONAL

Focus on the following Scripture passages this week during your quiet moments as you reflect on the person of Jesus.

> Day 1: Matthew 4:18–22
> Day 2: Matthew 11:25–30
> Day 3: Mark 6:7–13
> Day 4: Mark 8:14–21
> Day 5: John 5:31–47

# PROFILE: WHAT WOULD I HAVE NOTICED?

—————⚭—————

Movies about Jesus help bring him to life for me. As I watch these movies, and then return to the Gospels, I try to place myself in my familiar role as a journalist. What do I see? What impresses me? Disturbs me? How can I convey him to my readers?

I cannot begin where I normally begin in reporting a person, by describing what my subject looked like. No one knows. The key lies elsewhere. I move beyond physical appearance to consider what Jesus was like as a person. How would he have scored on a personality profile? Unlike many of the films about him, the Gospels present a man with charisma. He held the attention of crowds for hours and days at a time. He lived out an ideal for masculine fulfillment that nineteen centuries later still eludes many men. He cried in front of his disciples. He did not hide his fears or hesitate to ask for help. He loved to praise other people. He quickly established intimacy with the people he met. I doubt Jesus would have followed a "to do" list or appreciated our modern emphasis on punctuality or scheduling. He let himself get distracted by any "nobody" he came across. Jesus would accept almost anybody's invitation for dinner.

Jesus came to earth "full of grace and truth" (John 1:14). He spoke of God, who lavishes his grace on veterans and newcomers alike. Despite Jesus' emphasis on grace, no one could accuse him of watering down the holiness of God. Followers were drawn by the magnetic power of his words, which, in John Berryman's description, were "short, precise, terrible and full of refreshment." Jesus' statements about himself were unprecedented and got him into constant trouble.

Oddly, when I look back on Jesus' time from the present perspective, it is the very ordinariness of his disciples that gives me hope. Jesus does not seem to choose his disciples on the basis of native talent or perfectibility or potential for greatness. I cannot avoid the impression that Jesus prefers working with unpromising recruits. From such a ragtag band, Jesus founded a church that has not stopped growing in nineteen centuries.

### *Viewing Jesus on Film,* OPTIONAL, 10 MINUTES

Consider using clips from the following films as an opening to your time together.

*Oh, God!:* Just over an hour into the movie, John Denver meets with a group of theologians to discuss what he's seen. This meeting may resemble the kind of meetings that occurred in Jesus' day as experts tried to figure him out.

*The Greatest Story Ever Told,* tape 1: The scene of Jesus teaching his disciples by the road, at the forty-three-minute mark, shows the best and worst of this movie (great visuals, boring rendition). Also, at the one-hour mark, see the scene of Jesus teaching and healing in the synagogue.

*The Last Temptation of Christ:* Calling of the disciples, at the forty-one-minute mark.

*Godspell:* Contains many examples of Jesus' parables, jazzed up considerably, starting around the seventeen-minute mark.

*Cotton Patch Gospel:* "Who do you say that I am?" question is raised, at the seventy-three-minute mark.

*Jesus of Nazareth,* tape 1: Scenes of Jesus teaching, around the 105-minute mark.

*Jesus of Montreal:* Coming to terms with Jesus' life; various scenes beginning at the twenty-seven-minute mark.

*The Gospel According to St. Matthew:* Jesus' calling of the disciples, emphasizing the political dimensions, as seen through this Marxist filmmaker's eyes, beginning at the thirty-three-minute mark. Also, beginning at the fifty-five-minute mark, Jesus' disciples and others try to figure out his identity.

### Seeing Jesus through Scripture

As you read the following Scripture passages, give just a word or phrase to describe the emotions or personality characteristics Jesus displays.

Mark 6:30–31
Mark 6:34
Mark 1:40–41
Luke 10:21
Mark 3:1–5
Luke 19:41–44
Mark 14:34–36
Matthew 27:46
Luke 23:34
Luke 23:43
Luke 23: 46

### Looking at Jesus Within and Without, 25 MINUTES

If you are in a larger group, break into groups of four to six. Introduce yourselves if necessary. Discuss briefly with the group:

Have you taken a personality test? Which one? What did it say about your personality?

1. Why do most people prefer a tall, handsome, and, above all, slender Jesus? What do you think of the ancient tradition of Jesus as a hunchback or as a person suffering from leprosy? Can you imagine Jesus with some illness or physical deformity?

2. If Jesus took a personality test such as the Myers-Briggs Type Indicator, how would he be categorized?

   • *Extroverted* (focused on the outer world of people and the external environment; energized by what goes on in the outer world) or *introverted* (focused more on their own inner world; energized by their inner world)?

   • *Sensing* (tends to "find out" by using eyes, ears, and other senses) or *intuitive* (tends to "find out" by using intuition to learn meanings, relationships, and possibilities)?

   • *Thinking* (predicts the logical consequence of any choice or action; seeks an objective standard of truth) or *feeling* (considers what is important to you or to other people, without requiring that it be logical, and decides on the basis of person-centered values)?

   • *Judging* (tends to live in a planned, orderly way; likes to make decisions, come to closure, and then carry on) or *perceiving* (likes to live in a flexible, spontaneous way; seeks to understand life rather than control it)?

What is your conclusion? Does Jesus have a personality type? Are you the same personality type as Jesus? Explain.

Do you think of Jesus as "well adjusted"? Would most people in modern America?

3. If I had sought a one-word label to describe Jesus to his contemporaries, I would have chosen the word *rabbi,* or teacher. I know of nothing in the United States now that parallels Jesus' life. Surely his style had little in common with that of modern mass-evangelists, with their tents and stadia, their advance teams and billboards and direct-mail campaigns, their electronically enhanced presentations. Jesus' little band of followers, possessing no permanent base of operations, wandered from town to town without much discernible strategy.

What do you think Jesus would think of modern-day evangelistic crusades? What would he like about them? What cautions would he have? Do you know anyone today who chooses a lifestyle like that of Jesus?

4. What do you like about Jesus' parables (the parable of the good Samaritan, the parable of the prodigal son, and so forth)? What do you dislike? Do you find them powerful—or confusing? Why do you think Jesus told so many parables? (See pp. 94–95.)

5. Read the last two paragraphs on page 95, continuing to page 96. Jesus came to earth "full of grace and truth." He preached a message of God's grace—undeserved love

offered to everyone. He also proclaimed a truth more uncompromising by far than that taught by the strictest rabbis of his day.

Think of the church you grew up in, if you went to church. Did it emphasize grace or truth? Which do you display more of in your life—Jesus' grace or his truth?

Is it possible for Christians to overwhelm others with grace yet proclaim fully Jesus' truth? Can you think of anyone who does both?

6. Jesus didn't fit the pattern of other rabbis or religious teachers. He was not so much seeking truth as pointing to it, by pointing to himself. In Matthew's words, "he taught as one who had authority, and not as their teachers of the law" (Matt. 7:29).

As our study progresses and Jesus continues to point to himself, are you attracted to him? His personality? His message?

On pages 97–98 I describe the concentric circles of onlookers who followed Jesus around. Projecting back in time, where in those circles would you put yourself: close to the inner ring or out on the margins with me?

Do you have any prayer needs to share with the group?

### *Being Seen by Jesus,* 5–10 MINUTES

Spend this time in quiet prayer or meditation. You may want to reflect on the words Jesus repeated more often than any others: "Whoever finds his life will lose it, and whoever loses his life for my sake will find it" (Matt. 10:39).

You may also choose to take notes during this time. You can add on to the following prayer in the space provided or in your journal.

> *Dear Jesus, Y'shua, Redeemer, Son of Man, Mighty God, Wonderful Counselor, Emmanuel, Anointed One, the closer I look at you, the more I see in you—your complexity, your many sides, your simplicity, your depth. In myself I see reflections of you. I also see much that bears no resemblance at all. I despair of ever really looking like you, acting like you, being your hands and your feet. I still don't really understand you, so how can I hope to resemble you? Yet I'm not sure this is your intent. Do you really expect me to figure you out and methodically act like you? Maybe all you ask is that I let you do senseless things through me and leave the figuring to you. You seemed to love with a passion people who were ordinary. Just muddy, dark reflections. I know you're a Miracle Worker. And I believe that when I reach to you, you're reaching back, always reaching me. Make me yours. . . .*

THE JESUS I NEVER KNEW STUDY GUIDE

*Further Glimpses of Jesus*

- This week ask Jesus to do something in you or through you that is surprising.
- This week ask friends or coworkers of another ethnic background how they picture Jesus, both physically and in personality.

*Gazing on Jesus This Week,* Optional

Focus on the following Scripture passages this week in your quiet moments as you reflect on Jesus. Use these passages as your time allows.

> Day 1: Mark 14:32–34; John 11:32–37
> Day 2: Luke 17:11–19
> Day 3: Luke 14:1–4; 19:1–10
> Day 4: Mark 5:21–43
> Day 5: Luke 7:18–28; 10:17–21

# BEATITUDES: LUCKY ARE THE UNLUCKY

—⚬⚬⚬—

The Sermon on the Mount haunted my adolescence. I would read a book like Charles Sheldon's *In His Steps,* solemnly vow to act "as Jesus would act," and turn to Matthew 5–7 for guidance. What to make of such advice? Should I offer myself to be pummeled by the motorcycle-riding "hoods" in school? Tear out my tongue after speaking a harsh word to my brother?

Now that I am an adult, the crisis of the Sermon on the Mount still has not gone away. Though I have tried at times to dismiss it as rhetorical excess, the more I study Jesus, the more I realize that the statements contained here lie at the heart of his message. If I fail to understand his teaching, I fail to understand him.

When I covered the Beatitudes with my class at LaSalle Street Church, the Gulf War began and ended. As I prepared videotapes of Jesus delivering the Sermon on the Mount, General Norman Schwarzkopf was giving a briefing. Blessed are the strong, was the general's message. Blessed are the triumphant. Blessed are the armies wealthy enough to possess smart bombs and Patriot missiles. Blessed are the liberators, the conquering soldiers. The bizarre juxtaposition of the two speeches gave me a feeling for the shock waves the Sermon on the Mount must have caused among its original audience, Jews in first-century Palestine. "How lucky are the unlucky!" Jesus said in effect.

A few years later I attended a prayer breakfast at the White House with President Bill Clinton and eleven other evangelical Christians. We were given the opportunity to express our concerns. The question, What would Jesus say in such a setting? crossed my mind. Would he say, "Don't worry about the economy and jobs—the poor are the fortunate ones"? Or "Relax, sir, government oppression gives Christians an opportunity to be persecuted and therefore blessed"? I realized with a start that the only time Jesus met with powerful political leaders, his hands were tied and his back was clotted with blood. I came away from the experience puzzled afresh. What meaning can the Beatitudes have for a society that honors the self-assertive, confident, and rich?

To put the issue bluntly, are the Beatitudes true? If so, why doesn't the church encourage poverty and mourning and meekness and persecution instead of striving against them? What is the real meaning of the Beatitudes, this mysterious ethical core of Jesus' teaching?

I am not, and may never be, ready to declare, "This is what the Beatitudes mean." But gradually I have come to recognize them as important truths. To me, they apply on at least three levels.

1. *Dangled promises.* The Beatitudes are not merely Jesus' nice words of consolation to the unfortunates. It is a plain fact of history that for convicts in the Soviet Gulag, and slaves in America, and Christians in Roman cages awaiting their turn with the wild beasts, the promise of reward was a source of hope. It keeps you alive. It allows you to believe in a just God after all.

2. *The Great Reversal.* I have also come to believe that the Beatitudes describe the present as well as the future. They neatly contrast how to succeed in the kingdom of heaven

with how to succeed in the kingdom of this world. The Beatitudes express quite plainly that God views the world through a different set of lenses.

3. *Psychological reality.* The Beatitudes reveal that what brings us success in the kingdom of heaven also benefits us most in this life here and now. I would rather spend time among the servants of this world than among the stars. The servants clearly emerge as the favored ones, the graced ones. They possess qualities of depth and richness and even joy that I have not found elsewhere. Somehow in the process of losing their lives, they find them.

### *Viewing Jesus on Film,* OPTIONAL, 10 MINUTES

Consider using clips from the following films as an opening to your time together.

*The Greatest Story Ever Told,* tape 1: Sermon on the Mount, at the ninety-two-minute mark.

*Godspell:* A rendition of the Beatitudes, starting at the forty-four-minute mark.

*King of Kings II,* tape 1: The Beatitudes, at the eighty-five-minute mark.

*Jesus:* Sermon on the Mount, at the twenty-six-minute mark.

### *Seeing Jesus through Scripture*

The Sermon on the Mount is found in Matthew 5:1–7:29. In reading the following passages together, you will hear the Beatitudes and a selection of verses from the Sermon on the Mount. During this next week I strongly recommend that you read the entire Sermon on the Mount, as described in "Gazing on Jesus

This Week" at the end of this chapter (in the study guide). For this meeting read together slowly:

> Matthew 5:1–12, 14–16, 29–30, 38–42
> Matthew 6:1, 19–21, 25, 31–34
> Matthew 7:12, 13–14, 21–23, 24–25

### *Looking at Jesus Within and Without,* 25 MINUTES

If you are in a larger group, break into groups of four to six. Introduce yourselves if necessary. If you don't know each other, share something along this line: In what kind of dwelling do you live? An apartment? A house? A mobile home? Who is your most interesting neighbor?

1. If you have read the Sermon on the Mount before, how did you interpret it? Did you ever consider following it literally, such as by giving away all your money or possessions or by letting someone hit you a second time or by cutting off a body part? If you are reading it for the first time, what is your first impression of Jesus' words?

2. The trend today is self-help—learning to be assertive and independent, learning to show strength and confidence, learning to practice "tough love," learning to confront, learning to set limits, learning to manage finances wisely. In fact, much of the teaching on these subjects comes from respected Christian psychologists and writers. Many people have had radical, positive change occur in their lives due to these teachings. How do you reconcile this approach with what Jesus spells out in the Sermon on the Mount?

"But I tell you, Do not resist an evil person. If someone strikes you on the right cheek, turn to him the other also" (Matt. 5:39).

How does assertiveness fit with turning the other cheek? Do you think the same principle applies to word fights? For example, does Jesus call us to fight back with words, if not physically? How does he call us to speak (see Matt. 5:33–37)? Does that mean never speaking your mind? Does it mean being a doormat? Does it mean letting it appear that the other person has won? Read the second full paragraph about Gandhi on page 121 in the book. Have you grappled with this issue? Can you share an example? Can you describe someone you know who shows the power of "quiet strength"?

3. "Blessed are the poor in spirit, for theirs is the kingdom of heaven" (Matt. 5:3).

What does it mean to be poor in spirit? Which word would you choose from this list?

- Lonely
- Confused
- Remorseful
- Ashamed
- Depressed

- Needy
- Self-sacrificing
- Beaten-down
- Oppressed
- Another word _____

How do independence, strength, and confidence fit with being poor in spirit? How did Jesus embody strength? How did Jesus embody confidence? What does this verse say to the person suffering from low self-worth or from depression? To the person who has chosen a low-paying or unglamorous job? Read the second full paragraph on page 118 of the book, beginning with the words, "I was prepared ..." How have these issues become real in your life?

4. "Blessed are the merciful, for they will be shown mercy" (Matt. 5:7).

"Blessed are those who are persecuted because of righteousness, for theirs is the kingdom of heaven" (Matt. 5:10).

"So in everything, do to others what you would have them do to you" (Matt. 7:12).

What does it mean to show mercy to someone who has cheated you? To someone who has embarrassed you? What does it mean to show mercy to someone who has abused you, physically or emotionally? How does the tough love concept (setting limits as to how much one will tolerate in an unhealthy relationship with another) fit with finding blessing in persecution and doing to others as you would have them do to you? What is the value in showing mercy to the helpless? Read the last full paragraph on page 120, beginning with the words, "Then Nouwen ..." Have you struggled with these issues? Share an example from your life.

5. "Do not store up for yourselves treasures on earth, where moth and rust destroy, and where thieves break in and steal. But store up for yourselves treasures in heaven, where moth and rust do not destroy, and where thieves do not break in and steal. For where your treasure is, there your heart will be also" (Matt. 6:19–21).

"For the pagans run after all these things, and your heavenly Father knows that you need them. But seek first his kingdom and his righteousness, and all these things will be given to you as well. Therefore do not worry about tomorrow, for tomorrow will worry about itself. Each day has enough trouble of its own" (Matt. 6:32–34).

"Give to the one who asks you, and do not turn away from the one who wants to borrow from you" (Matt. 5:42).

What does Jesus say about money management? What would he say if questioned about IRAs and retirement planning or even health insurance? About saving for college? About a nest egg for emergencies? About spending wisely? About generosity in giving? How have you confronted this issue in your life?

Do you have any prayer needs to mention to the group?

## *Being Seen by Jesus,* 5–10 MINUTES

Spend this time in quiet prayer or meditation. You may want to reflect again on the words Jesus repeated more often than any others:

"Whoever wants to save his life will lose it, but whoever loses his life for me will find it" (Matt. 16:25). Do they have additional meaning for you after studying the Beatitudes?

You can take notes during this time if you choose. Or you can write a prayer in your journal or in the space provided.

### Further Glimpses of Jesus

- This week find out what your church or community is doing to serve the poor. Make plans to volunteer a couple of hours serving. Maybe others you are studying with would like to do this with you. As you serve, observe the poor. Are they blessed? How do you feel while serving?
- Review Monika Hellwig's list of the advantages of being poor, on page 115 in the book. Are these advantages or qualities true of the poor people you know? Plug in "I" in place of "the poor." Are these statements true of you?
- This week talk with someone who has experienced grief. If they are willing and able to share with you, ask them how God comforted them during their time of grief.

### Gazing on Jesus This Week, OPTIONAL

Focus on the following passages from the Sermon on the Mount this week in your quiet moments as you reflect on Jesus. Consider using Eugene Peterson's version of the New Testament in contemporary English, *The Message*, for your reading. Or use Clarence Jordan's *The Cotton Patch Gospel of Matthew* if you can locate a copy.

    Day 1: Matthew 5:1–16
    Day 2: Matthew 5:17–37
    Day 3: Matthew 5:38–6:18
    Day 4: Matthew 6:19–34
    Day 5: Matthew 7:1–29

# MESSAGE:
# A SERMON OF OFFENSE

———— ∞∞∞ ————

The Beatitudes represent only the first step toward understanding the Sermon on the Mount. Long after I came to recognize the enduring truth of the Beatitudes, I still brooded over the uncompromising harshness of the rest of Jesus' sermon. Its absolutist quality left me gasping. "Be perfect, therefore, as your heavenly Father is perfect," Jesus said (Matt. 5:48), his statement tucked almost casually between commands to love enemies and give away money. Be perfect like God? Whatever did he mean?

I once went on a reading binge in search of the key to understanding the Sermon on the Mount, and it brought some consolation to learn I was not the first to flounder over its high ideals. Throughout history, people have found canny ways to reconcile Jesus' absolute demands with the grim reality of human delinquency.

- Thomas Aquinas divided Jesus' teaching into two levels of commitment: precepts and counsels, or requirements and suggestions.
- Martin Luther interpreted the Sermon on the Mount in light of Jesus' formula "Give to Caesar what is Caesar's, and to God what is God's" (Matt. 22:21). "Christians maintain a dual citizenship," Luther said: one in the kingdom of

Christ and one in the kingdom of the world. The extremism in the Sermon on the Mount applies absolutely to Christ's kingdom but not to the world's.

- The Anabaptist movements chose a radically different approach. All such attempts to water down Jesus' straightforward commands are misguided, they said. They felt we should follow Jesus' commands in the most literal way possible.

- In nineteenth-century America a theological movement called dispensationalism explained such teaching as the last vestige of the age of Law, which was soon to be displaced by the age of Grace after Jesus' death and resurrection. Hence, we need not follow its strict commands.

- Albert Schweitzer, convinced the world would soon end in the apocalypse, saw the Sermon on the Mount as a set of interim demands for unusual times. Since the world did not end, we must now view those instructions differently.

Each school of thought contributed important insights, yet each also seemed to have a blind spot. Ultimately I found a key to understanding the Sermon on the Mount, not in the writings of great theologians but in a more unlikely place: the writings of two nineteenth-century Russian novelists, Tolstoy and Dostoevsky.

From Tolstoy I learned a deep respect for God's inflexible, absolute ideal. Like the Anabaptists, Tolstoy strove to follow the Sermon on the Mount literally. Sometimes he accomplished great good. His philosophy of nonviolence, lifted directly from the Sermon on the Mount, had an impact that long outlived him, in ideological descendants like Gandhi and Martin Luther King Jr. Yet his intensity soon caused his family to feel like victims of his quest for holiness. His wife said, "There is so little genuine warmth about him; his kindness does not come from his heart, but merely from his principles."

Tolstoy failed to practice what he preached, and he never found peace. He found, rather, that in many ways the gospel actually adds to our burdens. Yet to his critics he replied, "If I know the way home and am walking along it drunkenly, is it any less the right way because I am staggering from side to side! If it is not the right way, then show me another way; but if I stagger and lose the way, you must help me, you must keep me on the true path, just as I am ready to support you." Despite his failures, Tolstoy's relentless pursuit of authentic faith has made an indelible impression on me. Having grown up with many whom, in my arrogance of youth, I considered frauds, Tolstoy as an author accomplished for me the most difficult of tasks: to make Good as believable and appealing as Evil.

Tolstoy could see with crystalline clarity his own inadequacy in the light of God's ideal. But he could not take the further step of trusting God's grace to overcome that inadequacy. Shortly after reading Tolstoy, I discovered his countryman Fyodor Dostoevsky. He was the opposite of Tolstoy in every way, but he got one thing right: His novels communicate grace and forgiveness with a Tolstoyan force. Early in his life he was nearly executed but was spared at the last instant. He never recovered from this experience. He spent ten years in exile poring over the New Testament and emerged with unshakable Christian convictions. In prison he came to believe that only through being loved is a human being capable of love. He went on to write about grace in his novels. Alyosha, in *The Brothers Karamazov*, does not know the answer to the problem of evil, but he does know love.

These two authors helped me come to terms with a central paradox of the Christian life. From Tolstoy I learned the need to look inside, to the kingdom of God that is within me. I saw how miserably I had failed the high ideals of the gospel. But from Dostoevsky I learned the full extent of grace. Not only the kingdom of God is within me; Christ himself dwells there. There is only one way for us to resolve the tension between the high ideals of the gospel and the grim reality of ourselves: to accept that we will never measure up, but that we do not have to. We are judged by the right-eousness of the Christ who lives within, not our own.

Why did Jesus give us the Sermon on the Mount? Not to burden us but to tell us what God is like. He gave us God's Ideal to teach us that we should never stop striving yet also to show us that none of us will ever reach that Ideal.

### *Viewing Jesus on Film,* OPTIONAL, 10 MINUTES

Consider using clips from the following films as an opening to your time together.

*The Last Temptation of Christ:* Condensed version of the Sermon on the Mount, at the thirty-seven-minute mark.

*Jesus of Nazareth,* tape 2: Jesus debates the Pharisees, at the sixty-six-minute mark.

*Heaven:* Common ideas on "How to Get to Heaven," at the fifty-six-minute mark.

*The Gospel According to St. Matthew:* Unusual rendering of the Sermon on the Mount, beginning around the forty-minute mark. More at the fifty-six-minute mark.

*Jesus:* Selections from the Sermon on the Mount, including the Lord's Prayer, beginning at the fifty-two-minute mark.

### *Seeing Jesus through Scripture*

Read together the following passages:
Matthew 5:17–20; 7:7–12
1 John 4:19
Romans 5:20–21
Ephesians 2:8–10

71

*Looking at Jesus Within and Without,* 25 MINUTES

If you are in a larger group, break into groups of four to six. Introduce yourselves if necessary and tell the group: Do you see yourself as more of a perfectionist or as more easygoing? How do you think others see you?

1. You have probably reflected some on the Sermon on the Mount since the last meeting. As we get started today, read the following personalized list of the Beatitudes. How true of you are these statements? Choose one or two that you especially need to think and pray about. Discuss these with the group as you feel comfortable.

   • I am blessed because in my loneliness, my fears, and my inner struggles, God has promised me a beautiful future. That promise helps me see my struggles with new eyes.
   • I am blessed as I grieve. In the depths of my sorrow Jesus meets me and mourns with me, bringing comfort in unexpected ways.
   • I am blessed in choosing not to exalt myself. This means I get overlooked at times, but I'm living for God, not for the acclaim of men and women. Someday I'll be glad I chose the way of humility.
   • I am blessed in my yearning to live as Jesus did. God is faithful to me as I ponder Jesus' righteous ways and pray for the Spirit to guide how I live and who I am.
   • I am blessed because I choose to show mercy, even when others don't really deserve it. I see much in me that is undeserving, yet Jesus has been merciful again and again.
   • I am blessed because I'm careful about what I do, see, read, and think about. I want to be pure because this is

when I can see God most clearly. This is when I am closest to God.

- I am blessed because I long for peace among those around me. I desire to enter into the world of others to better understand and come alongside them. I'm willing to do what is uncomfortable for the sake of peace, following in the footsteps of Jesus.

- I am blessed when, because of my loyalty to Jesus, others look down on me, violate my God-given rights, lie about me with evil intent, or hurt me. This world is not my home, and persecution blesses me because it is a reminder of the kingdom of heaven that awaits me not so far away. For "no eye has seen, no ear has heard, no mind has conceived what God has prepared for those who love him" (1 Cor. 2:9).

2. Talk about your church background. If you went to church as you were growing up, what was the church like? Did it feel to you more focused on rules (for being good) or on grace (God's undeserved love)? How did this affect you? Does it still affect you today? If you did not go to church as you were growing up, did you have any religious influence in your life that impressed on you God's attention either to rules or to grace? Were your parents rule makers or grace givers?

3. As you have thought about the Sermon on the Mount over the last week, what have your feelings been? Frustration and helplessness? A desire to reach higher? Anger toward God for being unreasonable? Increased passion to follow

Jesus' words? A temptation to ignore them and get on with life? Which of these describes your response:

- "Get real! Does anyone really take all of this seriously?"
- "It's tough enough trying to be a Christian without trying to understand all this."
- "I'm encouraged. According to God's standards, I'm doing pretty good."
- "OK, God, let's give it another try. I really want to do this."
- "I've really blown it."
- "Amen! I need this reminder of how God sees things."

Look at the bulleted list at the beginning of this chapter (in the study guide) that describes various interpretations of Jesus' Sermon on the Mount. These are described in more detail on pages 134–36 of the book. What strikes you about these interpretations? Do any of them resemble your own line of thinking at one time or another?

4. How have you come to reconcile the Sermon on the Mount and Jesus' other hard teachings with your own life? What is your attitude toward striving to follow Jesus' way and resting in Jesus' grace?

5. Have you read anything by Tolstoy or Dostoevsky or seen films of any of their works? Review the summary paragraphs about these two authors at the beginning of this chapter (in the study guide), or review pages 137–42 in the book. Con-

sidering your life experiences, with which author do you most identify? How, then, does the other author speak to you? (Feel free to bring up other authors who make a similar point.) Have you ever read a book that brought you face-to-face with holiness or grace?

What good is good behavior without love (see 1 Cor. 13:1–3, 13)?

What good is love without good behavior (see 1 John 3:16–20)?

6. Do you agree with the last paragraph of the summary at the beginning of this chapter (in the study guide)? Does it agree with the Scripture passages you read at the beginning of today's study? How does the Sermon on the Mount leave you feeling?

Do you have any prayer needs you'd like to share with the group?

### *Being Seen by Jesus,* 5-10 MINUTES

Spend this time in quiet, individual prayer or meditation. You may want to reflect on the following words from 1 John 4:19:

"We love because he first loved us." Your meditation needn't involve a lot of thinking. You may want to simply repeat these words silently again and again, letting God instill them in you.

If you choose to write a prayer, you may add on to the following prayer in the space provided or in your journal. Or you can use this time to take notes on today's study.

> *Dear Jesus, your way seems hard—no, impossible—for me to follow. Yet you said, "My yoke is easy and my burden is light." The only way that can be true is if somehow you're living through me. But I need your help even in thinking this way. Convince me I can't do it on my own. I want to look like you. I desperately need your grace....*

### *Further Glimpses of Jesus*

- Make plans to read the book or rent the movie *The Brothers Karamazov* by Fyodor Dostoevsky. Think about how this novel can speak to our society today.
- Obtain a copy of the book *The Gospel in Dostoevsky* (Plough Publishing House of The Woodcrest Service Committee, Inc. Hutterian Brethren, Rifton, NY 12471). The book provides excerpts of explicitly religious material in Dostoevsky's works.

• Make plans to read a writing by or about Leo Tolstoy. *The Lion and the Honeycomb: The Religious Writings of Tolstoy* by A. N. Wilson (Harper & Row) is a good place to start. If you're ambitious, read any of his short stories or novels. Many collections are available.

### *Gazing on Jesus This Week,* OPTIONAL

Focus on the following Scripture passages this week during your quiet moments as you reflect on the person of Jesus. These passages tell us what God is like, and they give us an ideal to let Jesus enact through us.

Day 1: Matthew 5:1–16
Day 2: Matthew 5:17–37
Day 3: Matthew 5:38–6:18
Day 4: Matthew 6:19–34
Day 5: Matthew 7:1–29

# MISSION:
# A REVOLUTION OF GRACE

As my class in Chicago read the Gospels and watched movies about Jesus' life, we noticed a striking pattern: the more unsavory the characters, the more at ease they seemed to feel around Jesus. In contrast, Jesus got a chilly response from more respectable types. How strange that now the Christian church attracts respectable types who closely resemble the people most suspicious of Jesus on earth. What has happened to reverse the pattern of Jesus' day? Why don't sinners *like* being around Christians and the church today?

"You can know a person by the company he keeps," the proverb goes. Imagine the consternation of people in first-century Palestine who tried to apply that principle to Jesus of Nazareth. Jesus ate with a person known as "the Leper"; twice he allowed a woman to anoint him with oil while at a guest's home; he dined with at least two Pharisees; and he had dinner with at least two tax collectors. Why did Jesus make one group (sinners) feel so comfortable and the other group (pious) feel so uncomfortable?

Many first-century Jews preferred John the Baptist's stern message of judgment and wrath to Jesus' message of grace and a banquet spread for all. I can understand this odd preference for the law because of the legalistic environment I grew up in. Grace was slippery, but under law I always knew where I ranked. Similarly, the Jews were operating, in effect, by a religious caste system based on steps toward holiness, and the Pharisees' scrupulosity reinforced the system daily.

Jesus appeared in the midst of this system and had no qualms about socializing with children or sinners or even Samaritans. As Walter Wink noted, Jesus also violated the mores of his time in every single encounter with women recorded in the four gospels. Indeed, for women and other oppressed people, Jesus turned upside down the accepted wisdom of the day. Not only did he reach out to people of all groups, he proclaimed a radically new gospel of grace: to get clean, a person did not have to journey to Jerusalem, offer sacrifices, and undergo purification rituals; all a person had to do was follow Jesus. Jesus moved the emphasis from God's holiness to God's mercy.

In Jesus, God gave us a face, and I can read directly in that face how God feels about people who are poor, sick, or suffering unbelievable injustice. He answered the question of whether God cares. Jesus himself wept in his suffering. I find it strangely comforting that when Jesus faced pain he responded much as I do. He experienced sorrow, fear, abandonment, and something approaching even desperation. Still, he endured because he knew that at the center of the universe lived his Father, a God of love he could trust regardless of how things appeared at the time.

Jesus' response to suffering people and to "nobodies" provides a glimpse into the heart of God. God is not the unmoved Absolute, but rather the Loving One who draws near. God looks on me in all my weakness, I believe, as Jesus looked on the widow standing by her son's corpse, and on Simon the Leper, and on another Simon, Peter, who cursed him yet even so was commissioned to found and lead his church, a community that need always find a place for rejects.

### *Viewing Jesus on Film,* OPTIONAL, 10 MINUTES

Consider using clips from the following films as an opening to your time together.

*The Gospel Road:* Has the scene from John 8, of the woman caught in adultery, at the twenty-three-minute mark—an ideal scene for a country-and-western soundtrack. Also, at the twenty-seven-minute mark, the movie speaks of Jesus as a friend of sinners, and a dispenser of grace.

*The Last Temptation of Christ:* Strong scene on the woman caught in adultery, at the thirty-four-minute mark.

*Jesus of Nazareth,* tape 2: Prodigal Son parable, well told, at the beginning of the tape.

*King of Kings I:* Interesting twist on the woman caught in adultery, at the twenty-minute mark, with DeMille speculating on what Jesus wrote on the ground.

*Jesus*: Jesus dines with Pharisee, forgives sinners, is anointed by a prostitute, at the thirty-minute mark.

### Seeing Jesus through Scripture

Read together the following passages:
Matthew 9:9–13
Luke 7:36–50

### Looking at Jesus Within and Without, 25 MINUTES

If you are in a larger group, break into groups of four to six. Introduce yourselves if necessary. Share with the group: Do you wear perfume, cologne, or any other kind of scent? What do you like?

1. Can you remember a time as a child when you had a friend or group of friends who were not really accepted by others? Or perhaps you yourself felt like an outsider, a "nobody." How did it make you feel? When have you had this experience as an adult?

2. If you went to church as a child, what kind of people were welcome in your church? What kind of people feel welcome in the church you now attend? Why?

3. What do you think it would take for the "prostitutes," "tax collectors," and "Pharisees" of today to gather gladly in the church?

The story of the woman caught in adultery in John 8 reveals a clear principle in Jesus' life: he brings to the surface repressed sin yet forgives any freely acknowledged sin. How can we help each other to be "acknowledgers" of our own sin without being judgmental of others?

Review the paragraphs about Jesus' treatment of women and other oppressed people, on pages 154–55 in the book. Does the church today invite the involvement of women, various ethnic groups, the physically challenged, poor or low-income people, and other oppressed groups? What are the reasons when it does not?

4. In looking at the two Bible passages in this week's "Seeing Jesus Through Scripture," it is clear that Jesus affirms both mercy toward sinners (Matt. 9:9–13) and a genuine worship of himself (Luke 7:36–50). Are these key elements in your church's outreach?

How can a church communicate mercy toward sinners? Through its preaching? Through its community service? In its programs? In its worship service format? How?

How can a church encourage genuine worship of Jesus? Through its music? Through its preaching? Through its worship service format? Through the participation of lay-people in the services? Through its Sunday school, small groups, and other programs? Through its teaching on personal worship? How?

5. Review the incident with Greg in the book, on pages 147–49. An angry Greg says, "I feel like walking out of this place. You criticize others for being Pharisees. I'll tell you who the real Pharisees are. They're you [he pointed at me] and the rest of you people in this class. You think you're so high and mighty and mature. I became a Christian because of Moody Church. You find a group to look down on, to feel more spiritual than, and you talk about them behind their backs. That's what a Pharisee does. You're all Pharisees."

What groups might you be guilty of looking down on or talking about behind their backs to make yourself feel more spiritual?

6. Reversal lay at the very heart of Jesus' mission. As Japanese novelist Shusaku Endo sees it, Jesus brought the message of mother love to balance the father love of the Old

Testament. (See pp. 157–59 in the book.) Therapist Erich Fromm says that a child from a balanced family receives two kinds of love. Mother love tends to be unconditional, accepting the child regardless of behavior. Father love tends to be more provisional, bestowing approval as the child meets certain standards of behavior.

How does this idea fit with your personal images of God and Jesus? What kind of love did you receive from your parents? What kind of love do you feel you receive from God? From Jesus?

Do you have any prayer needs you'd like to express to the group?

## *Being Seen by Jesus,* 5-10 MINUTES

Spend this time in quiet prayer or meditation. In the Gospels, one person who loved Jesus showed it by anointing Jesus' feet with perfume. You may want to spend this time envisioning yourself in an act of pure, devoted love and worship of your God.

You may also choose to use this time to take notes or to write a prayer. Use the space provided or write in your journal.

## *Further Glimpses of Jesus*

- This week think about one thing you would like to have incorporated into either your church's worship services or its programming to better reach out to sinners or to better worship Jesus. Write a letter to your pastor or to your church leaders. Do this in a loving way, affirming them for their leadership. Before you write, pray. Be committed to supporting and assisting in carrying out your suggestion. Be patient if change isn't immediate.
- Make plans to visit another church whose worship service, programs, and/or community outreach is significantly different from your church's. Pray for a fresh vision of Jesus' presence through the church you visit.

## *Gazing on Jesus This Week,* Optional

Focus on the following Scripture passages this week in your quiet moments as you reflect on Jesus.

Day 1: John 3:1–21
Day 2: Mark 7:24–30
Day 3: Mark 14:1–11
Day 4: Luke 11:37–54
Day 5: Luke 15:1–32

# MIRACLES: SNAPSHOTS OF THE SUPERNATURAL

∾∾∾

As I was growing up, I envisioned Jesus as the Great Magician, and his miracles as magic. As I now reflect on his life, miracles play a less prominent role than I had imagined. Jesus' miracles generated excitement but not always faith. Why did he perform so few miracles? Why any at all? Why these particular miracles?

Jesus' first miracle was perhaps the strangest of all. For the first but surely not the last time in his public life, he changed his plans to accommodate someone else. He changed water into wine at a wedding. Perhaps with a twinkle in his eye, Jesus transformed those water jugs, ponderous symbols of the old way, into wineskins, harbingers of the new. The time for ritual cleansing had passed; the time for celebration had begun. Jesus' first miracle was one of tender mercy.

Miracles of healing captured the most attention. Jesus overturned common notions about how God views sick and disabled people. He denied that a man's blindness came from any sin, just as he dismissed the common opinion that tragedies happen to those who deserve them (see Luke 13:1–5). Jesus wanted the sick to know they are especially loved, not cursed, by God.

The only miracle that appears in all four gospels is the feeding of the five thousand, taking place on the grassy hills near the shores of Galilee. Here, after being miraculously fed in the middle of nowhere, the crowd intends to seize Jesus by force and crown him king. But he was not that kind of Messiah. His was a hard message of obedience and sacrifice, not a sideshow for gawkers and sensation seekers.

Jesus' last miracle, his raising of Lazarus from the dead, gives not only a preview of Jesus' future but also a compressed view of the entire planet. All of us live out our days in the in-between time, the interval of chaos and confusion between Lazarus's death and reappearance. Although such a time may be temporary and may pale into insignificance alongside the glorious future that awaits us, right now it is all we know, and that is enough to bring tears to our eyes—enough to bring tears to Jesus' eyes.

As I now read the accounts of selected miracles from Jesus' time, I find in them a very different message. In no event did the miracles bowl people over and steamroller them into belief. Otherwise there would be no room for faith. I now see miracles as signs rather than magic. Jesus' miracles did little to solve the problem of pain on this planet, yet through them Jesus showed that it was in his nature to counteract the effects of the fallen world during his time on earth. Miracles are early glimpses of the restoration of the universe.

As I have gone through all the Gospel accounts of miracles, I have come up with the following observations. These do not constitute a "philosophy of miracles" by any means. They are simply my personal observations.

1. The Gospels record about three dozen incidents of miracles, some of which were group healings. Although impressive, these miracles affected a relatively small number of people in one small corner of the world. Jesus performed no miracles of healing for the Chinese, for example, or Europeans. His miracles tended to be quite selective. Clearly, he did not come to solve "the problem of pain" while on earth.

2. Jesus resisted performing miracles "on demand" to prove himself, even when he had good opportunity to do so

(before Herod, with Satan in the wilderness, to impress doubters who were demanding a sign).

3. Jesus often hushed up his miracles, ordering people to "tell no one" about them. He seemed wary of the kind of faith miracles can produce: an attraction for the spectacular, rather than the kind of lifelong commitment he was after.

4. Jesus' miracles sometimes created distance, not intimacy. For example, when Jesus calmed the storm, the disciples in the boat with him drew back, terrified. Could this help explain why he interfered with nature so rarely?

5. People in Jesus' day found it no easier to believe in miracles than do people in our modern, skeptical age. For example, the Pharisees in John 9 worked hard to disprove the blind man's story. Similarly, they responded to Lazarus's resurrection by seeking another opportunity to kill him. Most astonishingly, the Roman soldiers who actually witnessed the greatest miracle, the resurrection of Christ, experienced no great change of heart—instead, they changed their story in return for a payoff.

6. Most miracles of healing came about because of Jesus' compassion, often because he was moved by the sight of a suffering person. Yet several times he fled from crowds who were pressing around him, demanding ever more miracles.

7. Spiritual miracles tended to impress Jesus more than physical ones. Remarkable or unusual faith impressed him most. When he healed a paralyzed man who was lowered to him through a roof, Jesus asked, "Which is easier: to say to the paralytic, 'Your sins are forgiven,' or to say, 'Get up, take your mat and walk'?" (Mark 2:9). Jesus' entire ministry provides

an answer. Physical healing was far easier, without question. Jesus knew that spiritual disease has a more devastating effect than any mere physical ailment. Why is it, I wonder, that many ministries are founded that focus on physical miracles, but I know of few organized to combat sins like pride or greed?

8. Jesus performed no miracles for the purposes of fundraising, fame, or self-protection. Unlike other miracle workers, he did not try to encourage mystery or wonder or appeal to a sense of magic. And denying his disciples' requests, he never performed miracles of retaliation.

9. Jesus also performed miracles to establish his credentials— so that when he declared who he was, he would have some evidence to back up the claim. "Even though you do not believe me, believe the miracles, that you may know and understand that the Father is in me, and I in the Father" (John 10:38).

10. Though they did not solve all problems on earth, Jesus' miracles were a sign of how the world should be and someday will be. They were, in fact, a preview of the future.

### *Viewing Jesus on Film,* OPTIONAL, 10 MINUTES

Consider using clips from the following films as an opening to your time together.

*Oh, God!:* About thirty-five minutes into the movie, John Denver challenges "God" to perform a miracle in his taxi and gets more than he bargained for.

*The Gospel Road:* See the miracle of the healing of the blind, at the fourteen-minute mark, or the miracle at the Cana wedding, at the eleven-minute mark.

*The Greatest Story Ever Told,* tape 1: Healing of the hemorrhaging woman, at the eighty-five-minute mark.

*The Last Temptation of Christ:* Casting out demons, and wedding of Cana, at the seventy-minute mark.

*King of Kings I:* Healing of the blind and the lame, with dispute about Sabbath healings, at the eight-minute mark.

*Jesus:* Calming the storm, healing a demoniac, and feeding the five thousand, at the forty-minute mark.

## *Seeing Jesus through Scripture,* 5-10 MINUTES

Read the following stories of Jesus' miracles, together or individually. Pay special attention to the message Jesus was giving through the miracle and to the response of the people to the miracle.

John 2:1–11
John 9:1–12
Luke 5:12–16
Luke 5:17–26
John 6:1–15, 22–36, 41–42, 60–66
John 11:1–50

## *Looking at Jesus Within and Without,* 20 MINUTES

If you are in a larger group, break into groups of four to six. Introduce yourselves if necessary and share briefly about whether you have ever experienced or encountered some kind of miracle—physical or spiritual.

1. What was your view of miracles as you were growing up?

- Magic
- A vending machine, with prayer as the coin
- Proof that Jesus was God
- The Devil's power
- Exaggerated stories

- The answer to human pain
- Jesus' opportunity to show he cared
- Other:

2. How do you view Jesus' miracles now? What is most thought-provoking to you as you review the list of my ten observations in the summary? Do you believe Jesus still performs miracles in the world today? Why or why not?

3. Jesus' first miracle was performed amid a wedding celebration and served mainly to keep the party going and spare the hosts from the embarrassment of running out of wine. It seems a strange way to begin using his miraculous power. Does God care about the seemingly insignificant things in your life? Can you recall a time when you sensed he did care?

How do you respond when people say that God helped them locate a parking place or find a lost object?

4. In Jesus' day, leprosy was dreaded in the same way that AIDS is today. Review the story on page 171 in the book, about the Indian man with leprosy who sobbed when a doctor became the first person in many years to physically touch him. Those with AIDS feel much the same way today. In light of Jesus' healing of the men with leprosy and paralysis, how would Jesus have treated AIDS patients

today? How can Christians show compassion for the physical distress of AIDS while also caring ultimately for the spiritual needs of those with AIDS?

Have you been through a period of sickness in which Jesus entered into your dis-ease of body, mind, and soul? How did he care for you?

5. An old Jewish tradition taught that the Messiah would renew Moses' practice of serving manna. When Jesus fed the five thousand, he merely whetted Jewish appetites. If this was the Messiah, they wanted more. It seems they were exhibiting our human tendency to set Jesus' agenda for our lives. When we see Jesus beginning to move, sometimes we're already writing the rest of the story and assuming he'll follow it.

Have you ever sensed yourself trying to set an agenda for God, telling him—rather than asking him—what to do?

6. The miracle of Lazarus sealed Jesus' fate. From that day on, people plotted to take Jesus' life. Yet he was willing to show his compassion and his power for the sake of the world he loved, knowing that it would take his own death and resurrection to conquer death for good.

In your own healing or in the healing or death of a loved one, how has Jesus' compassion and power been evident?

I wrote another book, called *Where Is God When It Hurts?*
Now when people challenge me to answer that question, I
respond with another question: "Where is the church
when it hurts?" How can the church, as the body of Christ
in the world, respond to suffering people as Jesus did while
on earth?

Do you have any prayer needs to express to the group?
Do you sense a need for a miracle in your life?

Unlike Jesus and unlike Lazarus, we have never heard the
sounds of laughter from the other side of death.

## *Being Seen by Jesus,* 5-10 MINUTES

Spend this time in quiet prayer or meditation. You may want
to reflect on Jesus' words to Martha after Lazarus's death:

"I am the resurrection and the life. He who believes in me
will live, even though he dies; and whoever lives and believes in me
will never die. Do you believe this? . . . Did I not tell you that if you
believed, you would see the glory of God?" (John 11:25–26, 40).

You can take notes during this time if you choose. Or you can
add on to the following prayer, writing in the space provided or in
your journal.

*Dear Jesus, you stand before me, assuring that if I
believe, I'll see the glory of God. My belief is the key. And that
is where I falter. I've seen your miracles and still I question you.
I've seen you care about the little things in my life. I know
you're my healer. You feed me body and soul. In questions of life
and death, I have only you to instruct me. Yet I continue to*

*question your love for me. I fear for my life and I worry about my needs. Your glory awaits, just around the corner in my heart. You've shown it to me so many times before. I do believe, Jesus; help my unbelief....*

### Further Glimpses of Jesus

- Watch for God's hand in unexpected places this week. What is God's message to you as he moves?
- Bring up the topic of miracles with family, friends, or coworkers. Ask others if they believe in miracles. Do those who believe in miracles believe in Jesus?
- **Note for next week's class:** We will be washing one another's feet next week, in remembrance of Jesus' foot-washing of his disciples. Please wear socks and shoes that are easily removable (no pantyhose!). Please come to class even if you choose not to take part. You will not be obligated.

### Gazing on Jesus This Week, OPTIONAL

Focus on the following Bible passages this week in your quiet moments as you reflect on Jesus. Use these passages as your time allows.

Day 1: Mark 9:14–29
Day 2: Matthew 9:18–26
Day 3: Matthew 9:27–34
Day 4: John 11:1–37
Day 5: John 11:38–53

# DEATH:
# THE FINAL WEEK

———— ∞∞∞ ————

The church I grew up in skipped past the events of Holy Week in a rush to hear the cymbal sounds of Easter. We never held a service on Good Friday. We celebrated the Lord's Supper only once per quarter. Yet the Gospels devote nearly a third of their length to the climactic last week of Jesus' life. Matthew, Mark, Luke, and John saw death as the central mystery of Jesus.

How can we who know the outcome in advance ever recapture the dire end-of-the-world feeling that descended upon Jesus' followers? I will merely record what stands out to me as I review the Passion story one more time.

*Triumphal Entry.* An adoring crowd makes up the ragtag procession: the lame, the blind, the children, the peasants from Galilee and Bethany. I imagine a Roman soldier galloping up to check on the disturbance. He spies a forlorn figure, weeping, riding on no stallion or chariot but on the back of a baby donkey, a borrowed coat draped across the animal's backbone serving as his saddle. Jesus wept as he viewed the city that could so easily turn on him.

*The Last Supper.* In Jesus' day, footwashing was considered so degrading that a master could not require it of a Jewish slave. In one act on an evening shortly before his death, however, Jesus symbolically overturned the whole social order. He washed the feet of his disciples. Hardly comprehending what was happening, they were almost horrified by his behavior. This act became one of three things Jesus asked his followers to do to remember him, with baptism and celebrating the Lord's Supper being the others. Following his example of footwashing was not easy for Jesus' disciples and has not become any easier in two thousand years.

*Betrayal.* As I read the Gospel accounts, it is Judas's ordinariness, not his villainy, that stands out. The Gospels contain no hint that Judas had been a "mole" infiltrating the inner circle to plan his treachery. Judas was not the first or the last ordinary person to betray Jesus. To Shusaku Endo, the most powerful message of Jesus was his unquenchable love even for—especially for—people who betrayed him. When Judas led a lynch mob into the garden, Jesus addressed him as "Friend." The other disciples deserted Jesus but still he loved them. His nation had him executed, yet while stretched out naked in the posture of ultimate disgrace, Jesus roused himself for the cry, "Father, forgive them. . . ."

I know of no more poignant contrast between two human destinies than that of Peter and Judas. Peter denied knowing Jesus three times on the eve of Jesus' death. Judas betrayed Jesus for thirty silver coins. Judas, remorseful but apparently unrepentant, took his own life and went down as the greatest traitor in history. He died unwilling to receive what Jesus had come to offer him. Peter, humiliated but still open to Jesus' message of grace and forgiveness, went on to lead a revival in Jerusalem and did not stop until he had reached Rome.

*Gethsemane.* By instinct, we humans want someone by our side in any great moment of crisis. I detect in the Gospels' account of Gethsemane a profound depth of loneliness that Jesus had never before encountered. Jesus was by no means powerless. But here he relived Satan's temptation in the desert. Either time he could have solved the problem of evil by force, with a quick stab of the accuser in the desert or a fierce battle in the garden. All this lay within

Jesus' power if he merely said the word. Yet as John Howard Yoder reminds us, the "cup" that now seemed so terrifying was the very reason Jesus had come to earth.

*The Trials.* Unlike a defendant in today's courtroom dramas, Jesus faced as many as six interrogations in the span of less than twenty-four hours, some conducted by the Jews and some by the Romans. In the end, an exasperated governor pronounced the harshest verdict permitted under Roman law. As I read the trial transcripts, Jesus' defenselessness stands out. Not a single witness rose to his defense. No leader had the nerve to speak out against injustice. Not even Jesus tried to defend himself. To the priests and the pious, Jesus represented a threat to the Law, the sacrificial system, the temple, and the many distinctions between clean and unclean. His claims about himself were too much. How could they be true? Jesus looked to be the least Messiah-like figure in all of Israel. Yet weak, rejected, doomed, utterly alone, only now does Jesus think it safe to reveal himself and accept the title "Christ," or Messiah.

*Calvary.* Even after watching scores of movies on the subject and reading the Gospels over and over, I still cannot fathom the indignity, the shame, endured by God's Son on earth, stripped naked, flogged, spat on, struck in the face, garlanded with thorns. Nothing—nothing—in history compares to the self-restraint shown that dark Friday in Jerusalem. With every lash of the whip, every fibrous crunch of fist against flesh, Jesus must have mentally replayed the temptation in the wilderness and in Gethsemane. Legions of angels awaited his command. One word and the ordeal would end. No theologian can adequately explain the nature of what took place within the Trinity on that day at Calvary. All we have is a cry from a child who felt abandoned: "My God, my God, why have you forsaken me?" (Matt. 27:46).

In a sense, the paired thieves crucified on either side of Jesus present the choice that all history has had to decide about the cross. Do we look at Jesus' powerlessness as an example of God's impotence or as proof of God's love? The cross redefines God as one who was willing to relinquish power for the sake of love. Power, no matter how well-intentioned, tends to cause suffering. Love, being vulnerable, absorbs it. In a point of convergence on a hill called Calvary, God renounced the one for the sake of the other.

### *Viewing Jesus on Film,* OPTIONAL, 10 MINUTES

Consider using clips from the following films as an opening to your time together.

*The Greatest Story Ever Told,* tape 2: Triumphal Entry, cleansing of the temple, and Pilate's interest in the disturbances are effectively portrayed at the beginning of the video. Also, at the forty-six-minute mark and at the fifty-eight-minute mark, Jesus is seen on trial and then carrying the cross.

*The Last Temptation of Christ:* Strong renditions of the Triumphal Entry, cleansing of the temple, Last Supper, Gethsemane, the Betrayal and trial, at around the ninety-six-minute mark.

*Godspell:* Gethsemane scene, at the eighty-eight-minute mark.

*Cotton Patch Gospel:* The crowd turns on Jesus, and the trial before Pilate, beginning at the eighty-seven-minute mark.

*Jesus of Nazareth,* tape 3: All the major events of Jesus' last week are portrayed, beginning at the thirty-five-minute mark.

*Jesus of Montreal:* History of the cross, crucifixion, at the forty-two-minute mark. Also, see the modern actor's delusions and the pietà scene, at the one-hundred-minute mark.

*King of Kings II,* tape 2: Trial before Pilate, with emphasis on political sedition, at the thirty-minute mark.

*King of Kings I:* DeMille's dramatic depiction of the Crucifixion begins at the ninety-seven-minute mark.

*The Gospel According to St. Matthew:* Pasolini gives a full account of the Crucifixion and events preceding it, beginning at the 105-minute mark.

*Jesus:* Most of the events of Holy Week are depicted, beginning at the seventy-minute mark.

### Seeing Jesus through Scripture

Read together the following passage:

John 13:1–17

### Looking at Jesus Within and Without, 20 MINUTES

If you are in a larger group, break into groups of four to six. Introduce yourselves if necessary and tell the group about your favorite pair of shoes. How long have you had them? Why do you like them so much?

1. Have you ever participated in footwashing before? If so, what was the experience like? How do you feel about washing one another's feet today?

2. How often does your church celebrate the Lord's Supper? What does this celebration mean to you?

3. Why do you think churches have ignored the literal practice of footwashing but continued to practice baptism and the celebration of the Lord's Supper? Although our feet

are usually cleaner today, does the ritual of footwashing still have value as a regular practice?

4. How does your church celebrate Holy Week, the week before Easter? Do you have a Good Friday service? A Seder dinner? A time for corporate prayer? A time of footwashing?

Have you ever given up a food or an activity for Lent (the forty weekdays before Easter, beginning on Ash Wednesday)? What have you or those you know done? Lent traditionally has been observed as a season of penitence. Today some Christians observe Lent rather in remembrance of the sacrifice Jesus made for us.

How do you personally remember Holy Week? How do you remember Good Friday? Do you work? Do you spend personal time with Jesus in reading or in prayer? Have you ever been to a Passion play or taken part in one?

5. Have you ever felt betrayed or abandoned? What were the circumstances? Share briefly and only as you feel comfortable.

Jesus wept as he rode on the donkey through Bethany. Approaching Jerusalem, he viewed the city that would soon turn on him and kill him. Later Jesus washed his disciples' feet in the Upper Room, knowing that Judas would betray him and that the other disciples would turn their backs on him. In Gethsemane Jesus' disciples slept through his agony. He surely must have felt as if God too had turned his back. Yet as he was betrayed, he called Judas "friend." In his last words on the cross, he forgave the men who had done the deed. He arranged care for his mother. He welcomed a shriven thief into paradise.

In these last days, Jesus must have felt like a parent watching his child about to make a horrible mistake. Or like a jilted lover watching his beloved leave him for someone else. Or like a child watching his father walk out when he was most needed.

In the midst of his intense pain, Jesus loved his betrayers more fervently than ever. Have you experienced this kind of "senseless" love for one who has betrayed you? Might this love be God-given? How does Jesus' handling of betrayal speak to your own experience of betrayal?

6. Why did Jesus have to die? If he came in similar form today, would the church and the government see him as a threat, too? Today the cross is seen everywhere—in jewelry and even in candy at Easter. Do you wear a cross? Has it ever seemed strange to wear a symbol of execution as adornment? What does the cross mean to you?

### *Being Seen by Jesus,* 15 MINUTES

[Leader: Come prepared with towels, basins (pots and baking pans will do), soap, and warm water. Lead the group in washing the feet of one another. Arrange the footwashing so that each person washes the feet of one who has not washed his or her own feet. This could be done in threesomes or as a large group in which each washes the feet of the person on the right. If you have access to Michael Card's *poiēma* on cassette or CD, have the song "The Basin and the Towel" playing during the footwashing.*]

We will spend this time washing one another's feet. (Feel free to refrain if you feel unprepared or uneasy.) This should be a quiet, reflective time. Silently ask Jesus and the Holy Spirit to speak to you and to inhabit this act of love toward one another. Remember Jesus' words: "Unless I wash you, you have no part with me. . . . Now that I, your Lord and Teacher, have washed your feet, you also should wash one another's feet" (John 13:8, 14). This act is symbolic of choosing the way of love and humility over power and prestige. It is a reminder of the attitude in which we can approach one another daily.

When everyone is finished, take a couple of minutes to discuss the experience. Did it feel strange? Awkward? Meaningful? If there is time remaining, you can write in your journal or in the space provided.

### *Further Glimpses of Jesus*

- Think this week about one thing you could give up if you chose to observe the next Lenten period. You could give up a food (chocolate), an activity (watching television), or a habit (smoking) to help you remember daily the sacrifice

---

*\*poiēma* by Michael Card (Sparrow, 1994).

that Jesus made, as you look toward the celebration of Easter and the victory achieved through Jesus' sacrifice.

- Pray this week about an act of betrayal you have experienced. Ask Jesus to help you see this betrayal through his eyes of fervent love. He weeps with you in your pain. He is also able to walk you through the betrayal and into a new morning of victory.

### *Gazing on Jesus This Week,* Optional

Focus on the following Scripture passages this week in your quiet moments as you reflect on Jesus. Use these passages as your time allows.

> Day 1: John 12:12–19
> Day 2: John 13:1–17; Luke 22:7–38
> Day 3: Mark 14:32–42
> Day 4: John 18:1–14, 19–24, 28–29:16
> Day 5: John 19:17–37; Luke 23:26–56;
> Matthew 27:32–56

# RESURRECTION: A MORNING BEYOND BELIEF

As a child, when my kitten Boots was killed by a dog, I learned the meaning of the word *irreversible*. Not so long ago, when three of my friends died in quick succession, the ugly word *irreversible* came flooding back. As I spoke at one of the funerals, I asked what would happen if our friend rose and appeared in the parking lot, alive again. That image gave me a hint of what Jesus' disciples felt on the first Easter.

The Gospels present the resurrection of Jesus as a shocking intrusion that no one was expecting, least of all Jesus' timorous disciples. Yet in their joy the disciples still took some convincing. We who read the Gospels from the other side of Easter, who have the day printed on our calendars, forget how hard it was for the disciples to believe. Jesus didn't make glamorous appearances but rather showed up in the most ordinary circumstances. He could always prove his identity, yet often the disciples failed to recognize him right away. Painstakingly he would condescend to meet the level of their skepticism, eating fish, inviting Thomas to finger his scars, instructing Peter in front of six friends.

That Jesus succeeded in changing a snuffling band of unreliable followers into fearless evangelists, that eleven men who had deserted him at death now went to martyrs' graves, avowing their faith in a resurrected Christ, that these few witnesses managed to set loose a force that would overcome violent opposition first in Jerusalem and then in Rome—this remarkable sequence of transformation offers the most convincing evidence for the Resurrection.

Although God allows death, I believe that he is not satisfied with such a blighted planet. Divine love will find a way to overcome. Because of Easter, I can hope that the tears we shed, the blows we receive, the emotional pain, the heartache over lost friends and loved ones, all these will become memories, like Jesus' scars. Scars never completely go away, but neither do they hurt any longer. We will have re-created bodies, a re-created heaven and earth. We will have a new start, an Easter start.

### *Viewing Jesus on Film,* OPTIONAL, 10 MINUTES

Consider using clips from the following films as an opening to your time together.

*The Greatest Story Ever Told,* tape 1: Lazarus's resurrection, near the two-hour mark.

*The Last Temptation of Christ:* Lazarus's resurrection, near the eighty-minute mark.

*Jesus of Nazareth,* tape 3: Scenes from Jesus' resurrection comprise most of the last fifteen minutes of the tape.

*Heaven:* Much on death, heaven, and the afterlife appears early on, at the twenty-minute mark, and after the forty-seven-minute mark.

*Jesus of Montreal:* Scene of Emmaus disciples, and those who discover the missing body, at the forty-seven-minute mark.

*King of Kings I:* Cecil B. DeMille introduced color to the screen with this depiction of the Resurrection, at the very end of the film.

*The Gospel According to St. Matthew:* Pasolini ends his movie with the Resurrection and the Great Commission.

*Jesus:* The events of the Resurrection, at the 110-minute mark.

## Seeing Jesus through Scripture

Read together the following passage:

Matthew 27:62–28:20

## Looking at Jesus Within and Without, 25 MINUTES

If you are in a larger group, break into groups of four to six. Introduce yourselves if necessary. Share with the group: Did you believe in Santa Claus as a child? For how long? How did you find out he isn't real?

1. People who don't believe the resurrection of Jesus actually happened tend to portray the disciples in one of two ways:

   • As gullible rubes (unsophisticated country fellows) with a weakness for ghost stories

   • As shrewd conspirators who conceived a resurrection plot as a way to jump-start their new religion

   Review pages 211–12 in the book. The disciples didn't show much gullibility. Rather, Jesus had to rebuke them for their unbelief (consider "doubting Thomas," their unbelief when the women came with the report from the tomb, and Matthew 28:17 in this week's "Seeing Jesus through Scripture"). The conspiracy theory falls apart, too, for if the disciples had set out to concoct a seamless cover-up story, they failed miserably. They cringed in locked rooms, fearing for their lives. Too afraid even to attend Jesus' burial, they left it to a couple of women to care for his body.

   What reasoning have you heard by others who doubt the Resurrection? How convincing are their arguments?

2. Have you ever doubted that Jesus was God's Son? Have you doubted the Resurrection? Do you still have some doubts? Feel free to share honestly. Most of us have doubted at one time or another. In fact, if we haven't doubted, it's possible that we've never really seriously thought about what we believe.

3. Astrophysicist Hugh Ross writes, in his book *The Fingerprint of God*, about discoveries involving classical thermodynamics, observational astronomy, and general relativity. Scientists have confirmed that the earth had a beginning point and therefore, according to Ross, must have had a "superior reasoning power" to initiate this beginning. In other words, God must exist. Yet upon this discovery, Albert Einstein would not accept the belief in a personal God.

> Two specific obstacles blocked his way. According to his journal writings, Einstein wrestled with a deeply felt bitterness toward the clergy, toward priests in particular, and with his inability to resolve the paradox of God's omnipotence and man's responsibility for his choices. . . . Seeing no solution to this paradox, Einstein, like many other powerful intellectuals through the centuries, ruled out the existence of a personal God.*

Perhaps Einstein could never get past his questions about God to take a look at Jesus. Yet others saw Jesus and still doubted. Clearly, people will find many reasons for reject-

*Hugh Ross, *The Fingerprint of God* (Orange, Calif.: Promise, 1991), 59.

ing both God and Jesus, with their reasoning being both rational and irrational. Rejection stems from both the mind and the heart.

Is Jesus' life, death, and resurrection enough truth to silence all doubts about God in your mind and heart? Why or why not?




How common do you think it is that those who doubt Jesus have underlying anger toward the church, such as Einstein expressed? Is this anger usually valid?



4. Madeleine L'Engle writes, in her book *Walking on Water,* "From Coleridge comes the phrase, *the willing suspension of disbelief,* that ability to believe which is born firmly in all children, and which too often withers as we are taught that the world of faerie and imagination is not true."*

Although much about the Resurrection invites belief, nothing compels it. Faith requires the possibility of rejection, or it is not faith. What, then, gives me Easter faith?

I believe in the Resurrection primarily because I have come to know God. I know that God is love, and I also know that we human beings want to keep alive those whom we love. I do not let my friends die; they live on in my memory and my heart long after I have stopped seeing them. Divine love will find a way to overcome. God will not let death win. Easter, to me, is a preview of ultimate reality.

---

*Madeleine L'Engle, *Walking on Water: Reflections on Faith and Art* (Wheaton, Ill.: Harold Shaw, 1980), 15.

What gives you Easter faith?

5. As you reflect on what gives you Easter faith, can you recall an Easter experience in your own life that resembled the joy of the disciples at Jesus' resurrection? Maybe hearing sudden good news, a diagnosis that turned out to be OK, a lost child or a pet that was found, or some similar experience.

Do you have any prayer needs you would like to express to the group?

*My soul sings your glory*
*And my spirit whispers your truth*
*My soul sings your story*
*As it mirrors the image of you.*
AMY ROTH, VOCALIST

## *Being Seen by Jesus,* 5-10 MINUTES

Spend this time in quiet prayer or meditation. You may want to reflect on Jesus' words in Luke 24:38–39:

"Why are you troubled, and why do doubts rise in your minds? Look at my hands and my feet. It is I myself! Touch me and see."

If you choose to write a prayer, you can add on to the following prayer in the space provided or in your journal. You may also use this time to take notes.

*Dear Jesus, Risen One. Hallelujah! You are risen indeed. Jesus, even as I rejoice, your life and death, your resurrection, are more than I can wrap my mind around. At times I'm tempted to take from you only what sounds good, what is easily accepted, and ignore the rest. But if you rose, you are God,*

*and as God all Truth is found in you. I may not fully under-
stand your Truth, but I'm finding that the closer I get to you,
the more I see that apart from you nothing makes sense. I cling
to Easter. I relish the telling of your story again and again.
Thanks for showing your scars. Thanks for remembering the
pain. Thanks for providing hope. Thanks that even when I
don't see you, you're as present with me as you were with the
two on the way to Emmaus. Keep walking with me. . . .*

## Further Glimpses of Jesus

- This week talk with family and friends about Jesus' resurrection. Ask if they believe it is true and whether they have
  ever doubted.
- Think about your typical Easter celebration. What do you
  do on Easter? Does what you do reflect the importance of
  the Resurrection and the fact that this day defines your
  faith? Can you think of ways to make this celebration more
  significant?

## Gazing on Jesus This Week, OPTIONAL

Focus on the following Scripture passages this week in your
quiet moments as you reflect on Jesus.

Day 1: John 14:1–14; John 15:18–27
Day 2: Mark 15:42–16:20
Day 3: John 20:1–31
Day 4: Luke 23:50–24:49
Day 5: John 21:1–25

# ASCENSION: A BLANK BLUE SKY

⸺ ∞ ⸺

If Easter Sunday was the most exciting day of the disciples' lives, for Jesus it was probably the day of Ascension. He, the Creator, who had descended so far and given up so much, was now heading home.

On the day Jesus ascended, the disciples stood around dumbfounded, like children who have lost their parents. They stood and gazed, not knowing how to go on or what to do next. Like the disciples' eyes, mine ache for a pure glimpse of the One who ascended. Why, I ask again, did he have to leave?

All along he had planned to depart to carry on his work in other bodies. Their bodies. Our bodies. The new body of Christ. The church, after all, is where God now lives. What Jesus brought to a few—healing, grace, the good-news message of God's love—the church can bring to all.

Four stories in Matthew have a common theme. An owner leaves his house vacant, an absent landlord puts his servant in charge, a bridegroom arrives so late that the guests grow drowsy and fall asleep, a master distributes talents among his servants and takes off—all these circle around the theme of the departed God. One more parable, of the Sheep and the Goats, directly addresses the question raised by the others: the issue of the absentee land-lord, the missing God. It gives a glimpse of the landlord's return on judgment day to settle accounts for all that has happened on earth. It also refers to the meantime, the time when God seems absent. We find that God has not absconded at all. Rather, he has taken on a disguise, a most unlikely disguise of the stranger, the poor, the hungry, the prisoner, the sick, the ragged ones of earth. God has designated the poor as his "receivers."

All through my own quest for Jesus has run a counterpoint theme: my need to strip away layers of dust and grime applied *by the church itself.* Many, far too many, abandon the quest for Christ entirely; repelled by the church, they never make it to Jesus.

Why don't we look more like the church Jesus described? Why do *I* so poorly resemble him? I offer three observations that help me come to terms with what has transpired since Jesus' ascension.

1. The church has brought light as well as darkness. In the name of Jesus, people like Saint Francis, Mother Teresa, Wilberforce, General Booth, Dorothy Day, and others—educators, urban ministers, doctors and nurses, linguists, relief workers, ecologists—have served all over the world for little pay and less fame. God's hands on earth have reached wider since the Ascension.

2. Jesus takes full responsibility for the constituent parts of his body. I take hope as I observe Jesus together with his disciples. Never did they disappoint him more than on the night of his betrayal. Yet it was then, says John, that Jesus "showed them the full extent of his love" (John 13:1), and then that he conferred on them a kingdom.

3. The problem of the church is no different than the problem of one solitary Christian. How can an unholy assortment of men and women be the body of Christ? I answer with a different question: How can one sinful man, myself,

be accepted as a child of God? One miracle makes possible the other.

Flannery O'Connor responded to a complaint about the church by saying,

> You are asking that man return at once to the state God created him in. . . . Christ was crucified on earth and the Church is crucified in time. . . . All human nature vigorously resists grace because grace changes us and the change is painful. Priests resist it as well as others. To have the Church be what you want it to be would require the continuous miraculous meddling of God in human affairs.

With a few exceptions, God, whose nature is self-living love, has chosen to allow himself to be "crucified in time" as his Son was on earth. Christ bears the wounds of the church, his body, just as he bore the wounds of crucifixion. I sometimes wonder which have hurt worse.

### *Viewing Jesus on Film*, OPTIONAL, 10 MINUTES

Consider using clips from the following films as an opening to your time together.

*Oh, God!:* "Why is any one person called to carry the Word?" John Denver asks about himself, at the forty-one-minute mark.

*Godspell:* Nice music—"Long Live God," "Prepare Ye (The Way of the Lord)," and "Day by Day"—at the end of the movie.

*Cotton Patch Gospel:* Are the disciples ready to take over? See the scene at the sixty-four-minute mark. Also, the Great Commission appears in the movie's final scene.

*Jesus of Nazareth*, tape 3: Jesus' great prayer for his disciples, from John 17, depicted around the fifty-minute mark. Also, the tape ends with the Great Commission.

*Jesus of Montreal:* Movie ends with striking metaphor of "Jesus'" body parts being distributed to others through organ transplants.

*King of Kings II,* tape 1: Summary of the disciples' attitudes, Jesus' instructions to them, at the one-hundred-minute mark.

*The Gospel Road:* At the fifty-five-minute mark, has an arty depiction of the death of Jesus as it impacts the world.

*King of Kings I:* One of few depictions of the Ascension on film, at the very end of the tape.

*Jesus Christ, Superstar:* Jesus' strength versus that of the Romans, at the thirty-minute mark.

### Seeing Jesus through Scripture

Read together the following passages:
Acts 1:1–11
John 21:15–23

### Looking at Jesus Within and Without, 25 MINUTES

If you are in a larger group, break into groups of four to six. Introduce yourselves if necessary. Share with the group: Are you afraid of flying? Have you ever wanted to Skydive? Parasail? Bungee jump? Have you done it or will you?

1. When have you felt like the disciples after Jesus ascended: gazing at the sky and not knowing how to go on or what to do next? Perhaps when you were laid off, ended a relationship, learned of an illness, lost a loved one? How did this situation require you to take on a new role or to make a shift in your thinking?

2. Read the third full paragraph on page 227 in the book, beginning with the words, "The first time ..." In the harrowing scene from Shusaku Endo's novel *Silence,* a Portuguese missionary priest, bound, is forced to watch as samurai guards torture Japanese Christians, one by one, and throw them into the sea. The samurai swear they will keep on killing Christians until the priest renounces his faith. "He had come to this country to lay down his life for other men, but instead of that the Japanese were laying down their lives one by one for him."

Jesus said to his disciples, "I am sending you out like sheep among wolves" (Matt. 10:16). When have you felt like a sheep among wolves in this world? When you feel this way, are you surprised or angry? Or do you struggle yet find comfort, knowing this is the way Jesus said it would be?

When you feel like a sheep among wolves, how do you typically respond? Do you move steadily ahead with your eyes on Jesus? Or are you tempted to adjust who you are and how you act, to fit more easily with those around you? Give an example. What would Jesus do?

3. Would it not have been better if the Ascension had never happened? If Jesus had stayed on earth, he could answer all our questions. I find it much easier to accept the fact of God incarnating in Jesus of Nazareth than in the people who attend my local church—and in me. Yet that is what we are asked to believe; that is how we are asked to live.

C. S. Lewis wrote,

> It is a serious thing to live in a society of possible gods and goddesses, to remember that the dullest and most uninteresting person you talk to may one day be a creature which, if you saw it now, you would be strongly tempted to worship, or else a horror and a corruption such as you now meet, if at all, only in a nightmare. All day long we are, in some degree, helping each other to one or another of these destinations.

The people you spend the most time with (friends, family, church, colleagues)—which destination are they encouraging in you?

Which destination are you encouraging in them?

4. By ascending, Jesus took the risk of being forgotten. The central question of the modern era is, Where is God now? By leaving earth and allowing his life to be lived through the church, Jesus accepted the probability of being forgotten by many. We who are so connected to our physical world—trees and telephones and fax machines—forget that the choices we make today bring delight or grief to the Lord of the universe.

When have you felt forgotten by someone? Have you had friendships in which this happened? Family relationships? What went through your mind as you realized you'd been forgotten?

God has taken on a disguise, a most unlikely disguise of the stranger, the poor, the hungry, the prisoner, the sick, the ragged ones of earth. Has God, in this disguise, ever felt forgotten by you? When is this most likely to happen?

Do you think the same principle applies to the visitor at church, the relative struggling financially, the college student nearby who can't cook, the prisoner in your city who doesn't get mail, your grandmother in the nursing home, or the rescue mission downtown that can't get volunteers? Do you tend to forget these types of "ragged ones"?

5. Many of us have heard the phrase, coined by Gary Smalley and John Trent, "Love is a decision." We know that not only is love an emotion, a warm feeling, but it's also a decision we make with our will. When we decide to love, we make a choice also to act in love whether or not the feelings of love are there.

Review the passage in John 21 from this week's "Seeing Jesus Through Scripture"—the painful conversation between Jesus and Peter. Could it be that Jesus himself was making the distinction between loving with the mind and will and loving out of spontaneous emotion? Perhaps Jesus was asking us to love others—the sick, the lonely, the poor, the hungry—by making a decision to do it, regardless of desire, as well as by acting impulsively and emotionally when the feelings prompt us.

What kind of a lover do you tend to be? Impulsive and spontaneous? Or thoughtful, planned, and consistent? Are you the same type of lover in a romantic relationship, with family and friends, and with acquaintances and strangers? How have you tried to show the type of love that doesn't come as naturally to you?

Is Jesus telling you anything about how he wants to use you as his hands and feet in the world? Tell the group if you're able, or keep the question in mind if you need more time to consider or pray.

6. In John 21:21 Peter asks, "Lord, what about him?" His response is classically human. Jesus has just finished speaking directly and personally to Peter, and Peter's mind goes immediately to the other guy: "If you're asking me to do this, what about him?" Jesus says simply, "What is that to you? You must follow me" (John 21:22).

Why is it that we are so easily distracted from God's words to us because we're looking at the lives of others?

When are you most likely to compare God's call to you with his call to someone else? Do you ever shy away from service to God because you're intimidated by someone else or simply don't see a place for yourself? Or do you avoid service because you don't see others in your life doing something as hard as what you feel God has asked you to do?

How can others, maybe even those in this group, help you find your place in Christ's body?

Do you have any prayer needs to share with the group?

First we meditate on Jesus, and then we go out and look for him in disguise.

MOTHER TERESA

### *Being Seen by Jesus,* 5-10 MINUTES

Spend this time in quiet, individual prayer, journaling, or note taking. You may choose to meditate on John 21:15–23. You may find it meaningful to pray the following prayer aloud together as a small group. You can add on to the prayer by writing in the space provided or in your journal.

*Dear Lord Jesus! Enable me to be more and more, singly, simply, and purely obedient to Thy service.....**

### *Further Glimpses of Jesus*

- This week commit to perform one act of love that is the opposite of the type of love that comes naturally to you. Be

---

*Adapted from a prayer by Elizabeth Fry. Quoted in Richard J. Foster, *Prayer: Finding the Heart's True Home* (San Francisco: HarperSanFrancisco, 1992), 71.

spontaneous if you never are, or plan a loving act ahead of time and follow through with it.

- I talk on the bottom of page 232 about the movie *Whistle Down the Wind,* in which three children meet a vagrant claiming to be Jesus Christ. They believe him and begin to treat him as if he really were Jesus. (Andrew Lloyd Webber has recently written a musical version of this movie.) Think this week about what it would be like for you to treat a needy person as "Jesus in disguise."

- This week think about the things you dislike about the church. Think also about the things you like. Talk with friends and family to get their opinions. What is your verdict? Are there more pros or cons to imperfect Christians living as the church, Christ's body, in the world?

### *Gazing on Jesus This Week,* OPTIONAL

Focus on the following Scripture passages this week during quiet moments as you reflect on the person of Jesus. Use these passages as your time allows.

> Day 1: Matthew 24:36–51
> Day 2: Matthew 25:1–13
> Day 3: Matthew 25:14–30
> Day 4: Matthew 25:31–46
> Day 5: 2 Corinthians 4:1–18

# KINGDOM: WHEAT AMONG THE WEEDS

---

Each fall the church I attended during my childhood sponsored a prophecy conference. Silver-haired men of national repute would sketch the movements of million-strong armies that would soon converge on Israel. Nuclear war would break out, and the planet would teeter on the brink of annihilation until at the last second Jesus himself would return to lead the armies of righteousness.

What sticks with me is not so much the particulars of prophecy as their emotional effect on me. I grew up at once terrified and desperately hopeful. Later, as I read church history, I learned that often before—during the first decades of Christianity, the end of the tenth century, the late 1300s, the Napoleonic era, World War I, the time of the Axis of Hitler and Mussolini—visions of the end times had bubbled to the surface. Each time, Christians went through a passionate cycle of fear, hope, and then sheepish disillusionment. The end times had not arrived after all.

In Jesus' day, Jews were poring over the same passages from Daniel and Ezekiel that would later figure so prominently in the prophecy conferences of my childhood. We disagreed on some details, yet our visions of the Messiah matched: we expected a conquering hero. "The kingdom of heaven is near," Jesus proclaimed in his very first message (Matt. 4:17), awakening the image of a political leader who would arise, take charge, and defeat the most powerful empire ever known. But to the crowds' dismay, it became clear that Jesus was talking about a strangely different kind of kingdom. Jesus announced a kingdom that meant denying yourself, taking up your cross, renouncing wealth, even loving your enemies. As he elaborated, the crowd's expectations crumbled.

Jesus never offered a clear definition of the kingdom; instead, he imparted his vision of it indirectly, through a series of stories. His choice of images is telling: everyday sketches of farming, fishing, women baking bread, merchants buying pearls. As I review the parables of the kingdom, I realize how far my own understanding has drifted from such homespun images. I tend to envision the same kind of kingdom the Jews did: a visible, powerful kingdom. I think of Constantine leading his troops, crosses emblazoned on their armor, with the slogan "By this sign conquer." I think of the drawings of armies marching across the bedsheets at the prophecy conferences. Obviously, I need to listen again to Jesus' description of the kingdom of God.

Those of us in the twentieth century, an era that has few literal kings, conceive of kingdoms in terms of power and polarization. We are the children of revolution. But Jesus' message of the kingdom had little in common with the politics of polarization. He invoked a different kind of power: love, not coercion.

Sheep among wolves, a tiny seed in the garden, yeast in bread dough, salt in meat—Jesus' own metaphors of the kingdom describe a kind of "secret force" that works from within. He said nothing of a triumphant church sharing power with the authorities. The kingdom of God appears to work best as a minority movement in opposition to the kingdom of this world. When it grows beyond that, the kingdom subtly changes in nature. In fact, problems seem to arise when the church becomes too external and gets cozy with government. As one U.S. legislative aide said after observing China's underground church, "They fervently pray for their leaders but maintain a careful independence. . . . I have seen more than a few [American] believers trade their Christian birthright for a mess of earthly pottage. We must continually ask ourselves: Is our first aim to change our government or to see lives in and out of government changed for Christ?"

In some important ways, the kingdom has not fully come. It is "Now" and also "Not yet," present and also future. Only at Christ's second coming will the kingdom of God appear in all its fullness. In the meantime we work toward a better future, always glancing back to the Gospels for a template of what that future will be like. We in the church, Jesus' successors, are left with the task of displaying the signs of the kingdom of God, and the watching world will judge the merits of the kingdom by us. We live in a transition time, marked here and there, now and then, with clues of what God will someday achieve in perfection. The reign of God is breaking into the world, and we can be its heralds.

### *Viewing Jesus on Film,* OPTIONAL, 10 MINUTES

Consider using clips from the following films as an opening to your time together.

*The Greatest Story Ever Told,* tape 1: At about the fifty-seven-minute mark, see the scene of Herod seizing John, and the contrast between various kinds of power.

*The Last Temptation of Christ:* Jesus and John the Baptist discuss love versus power, at the fifty-one-minute mark. Also, at the ninety-minute mark, Jesus and Judas discuss the options of leading a revolution versus being a suffering servant.

*Godspell:* Parable of sowing seed, at the fifty-three-minute mark.

*Jesus of Nazareth,* tape 2: The issue of the two kingdoms, of Zealots versus peacemakers, toward the very end of the tape.

*King of Kings II,* tape 1: Rather strange scene of Jesus visiting John the Baptist, and the contrast between them, at the one-hour mark. This is followed by the Romans' report to Pilate and Herod, bringing up the issue of two kingdoms. Also, Barabbas's different, violent method is depicted just after the one-hundred-minute mark.

### *Seeing Jesus through Scripture*

Read together the following passages:
John 18:36–37
Matthew 24:4–14
Matthew 13:24–30, 36–43

### *Looking at Jesus Within and Without,* 25 MINUTES

If you are in a larger group, break into groups of four to six people. Introduce yourselves if necessary and tell the group: Do you have a green thumb? What plants have you grown? What plants have you managed to kill? Do you have any horticultural secrets to share?

1. As a result of the prophecy teaching in my church as I was growing up, I felt both terrified and hopeful. In high school I took courses in Chinese and my brother studied Russian so that one of us could communicate with invading armies from either direction. My uncle went further, packing up his family and moving to Australia. I felt certain the world would soon end; nevertheless I banked all my childhood faith on the belief that somehow Jesus would conquer.

   How much have you read or heard about biblical prophecy? Who were the authors or teachers? Briefly, what was taught? What was your response? How did you feel? What action did you take?

Do you see renewed interest in prophecy, with the year 2000 upon us? Have you read a novel by Frank Peretti or a book by Hal Lindsey? If so, what feelings did the book evoke in you?

What is your response today to teaching on prophecy?

- I find it intriguing.
- It's an important part of the Bible, and I feel Christians are responsible for interpreting it as best we can.
- If we study the Bible carefully enough, prophecy can be interpreted accurately and can guide us.
- I find prophecy frustrating, so I avoid it.
- Prophecy frightens me, so I don't spend a lot of time with it.
- There are no modern-day prophets, so I feel it's useless to try to understand what only God knows.
- I feel the basics of prophecy are important, but trying to understand the details distracts me from living as Jesus taught.
- Other:

2. In a footnote on page 240 in the book, I say, "The Scribes who pored so assiduously over Old Testament prophecies did not recognize Jesus as the fulfillment of those prophecies. Should not their failure to interpret signs of the first coming sound a note of caution to those today who so confidently proclaim signs of the Second Coming?"

What is your response?

What meaning does Jesus' second coming have for you? Does it affect your life at all?

3. For a period of time I tried to read the Gospels through the eyes of liberation theology (the belief that God has called the church primarily to the liberation of all oppressed peoples, even if it requires violent revolution). Ultimately I had to conclude that whatever else it is, the kingdom of God is decidedly not a call to violent revolution. First-century Jews were doubtless looking for such an upheaval. Battle lines were clear: oppressed Jews versus the bad-guy Romans. But Jesus' message of the kingdom had little in common with the politics of polarization.

How do you feel about liberation theology? Do you think violent revolution is ever justified? What about the revolution of the Americans against the British?

4. People who looked to Jesus as their political savior were constantly befuddled by his choice of companions. He became known as a friend of tax collectors, a group clearly identified with the foreign exploiters, not the exploited. Though he denounced the religious system of his day, he treated a leader like Nicodemus with respect, and though he spoke against the dangers of money and of violence, he

125

showed love and compassion toward a rich young ruler and a Roman centurion.

Jesus honored the dignity of people, whether he agreed with them or not. The person was more important than any category or label.

Can you recall a time when you were treated by another with disapproval because they felt you weren't spiritual enough? Were they right? How did this treatment affect you?

Can you think of anyone you treat with disapproval, as a category rather than a person? (Out of sensitivity to others, you may choose to reflect silently on this question rather than discuss it with the group.)

5. How easy it is to join the politics of polarization, to find myself shouting across the picket lines at the "enemy" on the other side. Regardless of the merits of a given issue, political movements risk pulling onto themselves the mantle of power that smothers love. From Jesus I learn that whatever activism I get involved in, it must not drive out love and humility; otherwise I betray the kingdom of heaven. (See p. 245 in the book.)

Christians throughout the centuries have been leaders in proclaiming truth in ethics and morality. Yet these same Christians have often struggled in leading the way with love and humility. If you strongly disagree with someone—say on a controversial issue such as abortion, homosexuality, or capital punishment—how can you continue to treat them with dignity? (Don't let this discussion become focused on political specifics. That will distract us. Focus instead on practical ways you can maintain love and humility even while sharply disagreeing with others.)

Read the last three paragraphs on page 246 in the book, beginning with the words, "Despite Jesus' plain example . . ." Do you agree? What do you see happening in our nation as Christians take a political voice?

6. Turn to the parable about the wheat and weeds in Matthew 13. Look at the parable and at the explanation. Envision yourself, if you believe in Jesus, as wheat amid weeds in a vast field. Notice the language Jesus used in the explanation of the parable. He talks of sin and evil and burning fire. If Jesus speaks so strongly about those whom the weeds represent, he must take seriously the wrongs we encounter. Notice also that the wheat survives until the harvest.

Take a moment as a small group or as a large group to lay hands on one another and pray for the strength to live as wheat among weeds in the world. Pray that our lives would not focus so much on containing the weeds that in an attempt to pull them, we also destroy the growth of the gospel. Pray for love and humility, that we may shine for God's kingdom here on earth as we wait eagerly for Jesus' return.

## *Being Seen by Jesus,* 5–10 MINUTES

Spend this time in quiet, individual prayer, meditation, journaling, or note taking. You may want to reflect on Jesus' prayer in John 17:17–19:

"Sanctify them by the truth; your word is truth. As you sent me into the world, I have sent them into the world. For them I sanctify myself, that they too may be truly sanctified."

Sanctification is a term we don't talk about in our churches a lot anymore. Oswald Chambers says, "Sanctification means being made one with Jesus so that the disposition that ruled Him will rule us.... It is not a question of whether God is willing to sanctify me; is it my will? Am I willing to let God do in me all that has been made possible by the Atonement?"*

You may choose to meditate instead on Jesus' words a little later, in John 17:20–23:

My prayer is not for them alone. I pray also for those who will believe in me through their message, that all of them may be one, Father, just as you are in me and I am in you. May they also be in us so that the world may believe that you have sent me. I have given them the glory that you gave me, that they may be one as we are one: I in them and you in me. May they be brought to complete unity to let the world know that you sent me and have loved them even as you have loved me.

If you choose, you can write a prayer in your journal or in the space provided.

---

*Oswald Chambers, *My Utmost for His Highest* (New York: Dodd, Mead & Co., 1963), 39, 294 (February 8, October 20).

### Further Glimpses of Jesus

- Choose one political cause you feel is important. Spend time in prayer this week, asking God to direct your involvement in this cause. Each time you pray, commit to a physical posture of hands open, palms facing upward, releasing your cause and yourself to God.
- Find someone who is actively involved in the political arena or actively working for a political cause. Talk with them about the ideas discussed in today's session. Ask for their thoughts. Be loving and sensitive, careful not to criticize. Through loving, respect-filled conversation, we can all continue to learn and grow.

### Gazing on Jesus This Week, OPTIONAL

Focus on the following Scripture passages this week during your quiet moments as you reflect on the person of Jesus. Use these passages as your time allows.

Day 1: Matthew 13:1–23
Day 2: Matthew 13:31–35, 44–46
Day 3: Matthew 13:47–52
Day 4: Matthew 5:13–16
Day 5: Matthew 10:5–42

# THE
# DIFFERENCE HE MAKES

———— ∞∞∞ ————

I conclude my survey of Jesus with as many questions as answers. I now have a built-in suspicion against all attempts to categorize Jesus, to box him in. Jesus is radically unlike anyone else who has ever lived. The difference, in Charles Williams's phrase, is the difference between "one who is an example of living and one who is the life itself."

To sum up what I have learned about Jesus, I offer a series of impressions. They do not form a whole picture by any means, but these are the facets of Jesus' life that challenge me and, I suspect, will never cease to challenge me.

*A Sinless Friend of Sinners.* When Jesus came to earth, demons recognized him, the sick flocked to him, and sinners doused his feet and head with perfume. Meanwhile he offended pious Jews with their strict preconceptions of what God should be like. Their rejection makes me wonder: Could religious types be doing just the reverse now? Could we be perpetuating an image of Jesus that fits our pious expectations but does not match the person portrayed so vividly in the Gospels?

Jesus was a friend of sinners. Yet Jesus himself was not a sinner. I view with amazement Jesus' uncompromising blend of graciousness toward sinners and hostility toward sin, because in much of church history I see virtually the opposite. For example, nowadays many of the same Christians who hotly condemn homosexuality, which Jesus did not mention, disregard his straightforward commands against divorce. All too often sinners feel unloved by a church that, in turn, keeps altering its definition of sin—exactly the opposite of Jesus' pattern. Something has gone awry.

*The God-Man.* Jesus' audacious claims about himself—"I and the Father are one" (John 10:30)—pose what may be the central problem of all history, the dividing point between Christianity and other religions. Although Muslims—and, increasingly, Jews—respect Jesus as a great teacher and prophet, no Muslim can imagine Mohammed claiming to be Allah, any more than a Jew can imagine Moses claiming to be Yahweh. Hindus believe in many incarnations but not one Incarnation, while Buddhists have no categories in which to conceive of a sovereign God becoming a human being.

Could Jesus' disciples have backfilled his teaching to include such brazen claims, as part of their conspiracy to launch a new religion? Unlikely. The disciples were inept conspirators, and in fact the Gospels portray them as resistant to the very idea of Jesus' divinity. Yet by the time the Gospels were written, the disciples regarded Jesus as the Word who was God, through whom all things were made. As I have studied the Gospels, I have come to agree with C. S. Lewis, who wrote, in a famous passage in *Mere Christianity,*

> A man who was merely a man and said the sort of things Jesus said would not be a great moral teacher. He would either be a lunatic—on the level with the man who says he is a poached egg—or else he would be the Devil of Hell. You must make your choice. Either this man was, and is, the Son of God; or else a madman or something worse. (*Mere Christianity,* 56)

*Portrait of God.* George Buttrick, former chaplain at Harvard, recalls that students would come into his office and declare, "I don't believe in God." Buttrick would give this disarming reply: "Sit down and tell me what kind of God you don't believe in. I probably don't believe in that God either." And then he would talk about Jesus, the corrective to all our assumptions about God.

Martin Luther encouraged his students to flee the hidden God and run to Christ, and now I know why. If I use a magnifying glass to examine a fine painting, the object in the center of the glass stays crisp and clear, while around the edges the view grows increasingly distorted. For me, Jesus has become the focal point. When I speculate about such imponderables as the problem of pain or providence versus free will, everything becomes fuzzy. But if I look at Jesus himself, at how he treated actual people in pain, at his calls to free and diligent action, clarity is restored. I can worry myself into a state of spiritual ennui over questions like, "What good does it do to pray if God already knows everything?" Jesus silences such questions: he prayed; so should we.

*The Lover.* Jesus reveals a God who comes in search of us, a God who makes room for our freedom even when it costs the Son's life, a God who is vulnerable. Above all, Jesus reveals a God who is love. Love has never been a normal way of describing what happens between human beings and their God. Not once does the Qur'an apply the word love to God. Aristotle stated bluntly, "It would be eccentric for anyone to claim that he loved Zeus." In dazzling contrast, the Christian Bible affirms, "God is love" (1 John 4:16) and cites love as the main reason Jesus came to earth: "This is how God showed his love among us: He sent his one and only Son into the world that we might live through him" (1 John 4:9).

I remember a long night in O'Hare Airport, waiting impatiently for a flight that was delayed for five hours. I happened to be next to a wise woman who was traveling to the same conference. I was writing the book *Disappointment with God* at the time, and I felt burdened by other people's pains and sorrows, doubts and unanswered prayers. My companion listened to me in silence for a very long time, and then out of nowhere she asked a question that has always stayed with me. "Philip, do you ever just let God love you?" she said. "It's pretty important, I think." I realized with a start that she had brought to light a gaping hole in my spiritual life. For all my absorption in the Christian faith, I had missed the most important message of all. The story of Jesus is a story of celebration, a story of love. Jesus embodies the promise of a God who will go to any length to win us back. Not the least of Jesus' accomplishments is that he made us somehow lovable to God.

*Portrait of Humanity.* When a light is brought into a room, what was a window becomes also a mirror reflecting back the contents of that room. In Jesus not only do we have a window to God, we also have a mirror of ourselves. Human beings were, after all, created in the image of God; Jesus reveals what that image should look like.

God's character did not permit the option of simply declaring about this defective planet, "It doesn't matter." God's Son had to encounter evil personally in a way that perfect deity had never before encountered evil. He had to forgive sin by taking on our sin. He had to defeat death by dying. He had to learn sympathy for human beings by becoming one. Because of the Incarnation, Hebrews implies, God hears our prayers in a new way, having lived here and having prayed as a weak and vulnerable human being.

*The Wounded Healer.* The author and preacher Tony Campolo delivers a stirring sermon adapted from an elderly black pastor at his church in Philadelphia. "It's Friday, but Sunday's Comin'" is the title of the sermon, and once you know the title, you know the whole sermon. The disciples who lived through both days, Friday and Sunday, never doubted God again. They had learned that when God seems most absent, he may be closest of all; when God looks most powerless, he may be most powerful; when God looks most dead, he may be coming back to life.

Campolo skipped one day in his sermon, though. The other two days have earned names on the church calendar: Good Friday and Easter Sunday. Yet in a real sense, we live on Saturday, the day with no name. What the disciples experienced on a small scale—three days in grief over one man who had died on a cross—we now live through on a cosmic scale. Human history grinds on between the time of promise and fulfillment. Easter opened up a crack in a decaying universe, sealing the promise that someday God will enlarge the miracle of Easter to a cosmic scale.

### *Viewing Jesus on Film,* OPTIONAL, 10 MINUTES

Consider using clips from the following films as an opening to your time together.

*The Last Temptation of Christ:* Jesus argues with a rabbi and claims divinity, at the eighty-seven-minute mark.

*Jesus of Montreal:* Actress discusses how Jesus "got to her," at the ninety-minute mark. Contrast this to a cynical priest's attitude, just preceding this scene.

*King of Kings I:* Actually depicts the rending of the temple veil, about the one-hundred-minute mark.

*Jesus:* One of the few depictions of the Transfiguration, at the forty-nine-minute mark.

*Jesus Christ, Superstar:* Mary and Judas give contrasting reactions to Jesus, at the twenty-minute mark.

### *Seeing Jesus through Scripture*

Read together the following passages:
John 14:5–14
Hebrews 4:14–16; 10:35–39

### *Looking at Jesus Within and Without,* 25 MINUTES

If you are in a larger group, break into groups of four to six. Introduce yourselves if necessary and tell the group about the friend you've known the longest. How long have you been friends? In what ways has your friendship undergone change?

1. In one of his earlier books, Salman Rushdie said that in the true battle of history, the pendulum swings back and forth between those who say, "Anything goes," and those who say, "Oh, no you don't!" As part of this history, the church has moved away from the divine balance Jesus set out for us. Every time the church has tried to legislate a form of Christian morality, it has found it hard to communicate grace.

   Are you and those in your life more concerned with guarding Christian standards or giving Christlike love?

   What have you found to be most difficult in balancing out a love for holiness with a lifestyle of grace?

2. Think about the statement made by chaplain George Buttrick in the paragraph titled "Portrait of God" in the summary at the beginning of this session. Buttrick said, "Tell me what kind of God you don't believe in. I probably don't believe in that God either."

   What has been your biggest complaint about God, now or in the past? How does the person of Jesus speak to that complaint?

3. If I were to ask you, "Do you ever just let God love you?" what would you say? Do you tend to focus more on doing for God, thinking about God's commands, expressing love to God, or receiving love from God?

How can a person make a practice of letting God love him or her?

4. During that wrinkle in time known as the Incarnation, God experienced what it is like to be a human being. In thirty-three years on earth, God's Son learned about poverty and family squabbles and social rejection and verbal abuse and betrayal and pain. He encountered evil personally, in a way that perfect deity had never before encountered evil. He had to forgive sins by taking on our sin. He had to defeat death by dying. He had to learn sympathy for human beings by becoming one.

   How does this idea, found on page 271 in the book, fit with your understanding of God? Does the thought of God knowing and loving you in a deeper way because of Jesus change your relationship with God?

5. On page 272 in the book, I tell about a walk I took in Bombay, where I saw worship centers of the four major world religions. Here is what I observed.

   • Hindu temples: Carved, brightly painted images depicted some of the thousands of gods and goddesses in the Hindu pantheon.
   • Muslim mosque: A soaring spire pointed skyward, toward Allah.
   • Buddhist center: A gilded statue of Buddha smiled, expressing the belief that the key to contentment lies in developing inner strength that allows one to surmount any suffering in life.

- Christian church: Atop the spire above the church stood a large, ornate cross.

Was there a time in your life when you called yourself a Christian only because it was your family's religion? Or because it was your friends' religion? Or because you hadn't really considered anything else? How has the Cross taken on new meaning during your study of Jesus these fourteen weeks? How does the Cross make Christianity distinct from other religions?

6. As you think back on your time with this group and with Jesus over the last fourteen weeks, what stands out in your mind? What ideas or activities will you most remember? What new insights about Jesus impacted you most? How have you seen people in your group change? What feelings toward Jesus will you carry away with you?

Do you have any prayer needs to express to the group in this last meeting?

Jesus is radically unlike anyone else who has ever lived.

### *Being Seen by Jesus,* 5–10 MINUTES

Spend this time in quiet prayer or meditation. You may want to reflect on Jesus' words in John 14:12: "I tell you the truth, anyone who has faith in me will do what I have been doing. He will do even greater things than these, because I am going to the Father."

Or you may choose to reflect on Jesus' words in John 15:9:

"As the Father has loved me, so have I loved you. Now remain in my love."

You may want to simply sit quietly with your eyes closed, letting God love you. Sit with Jesus and enjoy his love, just as you would sit in silence with a loved one.

If you have never asked Jesus to walk with you and acknowledged him as your Savior, this would be a good time. Those who follow Jesus should bear his "family likeness." Has Jesus changed your life through this study? Do you believe he lived on earth, died because he loved you, and rose again to give you life forever with him? If so, why not ask him to enter your life right now? Simply thank him for what he has done, accept his love, and ask him to begin the process of forming you into the kind of person he wants you to be.

You can add on to the following prayer in the space provided or in your journal. This can also be done at a later time if you choose to sit quietly now.

> *Dear Jesus, my head is swimming but my eyes are clearer. I can't escape you. I don't think I want to. I can't go back to who I was before, and I'm not sure how to go forward. But I am not alone. You love me; God loves me. You are what I need. Powerful. Human. True. Friend. Wounded. Holy. Love. God. Thank you, Jesus....*

### *Further Glimpses of Jesus*

- This week be conscious of letting Jesus love you. In much the same way you would enjoy a sunset or a soak in the tub or a walk hand in hand, sit and let Jesus love you. Words aren't needed, but if something comes to mind, keep your prayers short and simple. Don't let your concerns rob you of this time to receive Jesus' love. This practice might feel strange at first, but if you stay with it, you may find Jesus transforming you and other relationships.
- Spend time flipping through this study guide and the book *The Jesus I Never Knew*. Reread your notes, prayers, and the passages that particularly impacted you. If you kept a journal, read through your entries. Ask Jesus to continue the work he's begun in you.

### *Gazing on Jesus This Week,* OPTIONAL

Focus on the following Scripture passages this week in your quiet moments as you reflect on Jesus. Use these passages as your time allows.

Day 1: John 14:1–14
Day 2: John 14:15–31
Day 3: John 15:1–17
Day 4: John 16:17–33
Day 5: Hebrews 10:1–25

# MOVIE APPENDIX

Where can you obtain the following videos? If they are still in current release, you can order most of them through a large video chain, such as Blockbuster. They usually have a catalog of "films in print." More obscure films can be found through an "art film" distributor, such as Facets Video in Chicago (1-800-331-6197). Explicitly Christian films may be ordered at your local Christian bookstore or obtained through a distributor such as Gospel Films (call 1-800-253-0413 or contact them at http://www.gospelcom.net/gf/ on the Internet). Gateway Films is another outlet (1-800-523-0226). Several Catholic distributors have good supplies of videos as well, so you may want to contact a Catholic school or library for leads. (Try Ignatius Press at 1-800-651-1531.)

These are some of the movies I showed my class, listed in order of their potential usefulness to you.

*Jesus of Nazareth:* This film by Franco Zefferelli, shown several times on network television, is the most realistic, faithful rendering of Jesus' life on film. Many scenes have great power. The complete movie takes up three videos and covers most of the major events of Jesus' life. Many large video chains have this film available for rental.

*Jesus:* A one-video presentation of Jesus' life sponsored by Campus Crusade for Christ, this film has been shown to hundreds of millions of people around the world, serving as many people's first introduction to Jesus. Because of their missionary emphasis, Campus Crusade may well encourage showing clips from this film, waiving copyright restrictions. Most major cities have a Campus Crusade office, or your local Christian bookstore may know how to order this film.

*The Visual Bible:* I have not graphed out individual scenes of this production, so you will not find scenes referred to in the chapter-by-chapter meetings. It is a new, lavish production, very faithful to biblical texts. The gospel of Matthew has been released in three volumes; Acts will soon be available. Like Campus Crusade, the owners of this film may be willing to accommodate requests for more lenient copyright restrictions. Write Gener8Xion Entertainment, Inc., P.O. Box 6548-347, Orange, CA 92613 or call 1-800-332-4253.

*The Greatest Story Ever Told:* In an incredible miscasting, this movie features Max van Sydow in the lead role, so Jesus speaks with a thick Scandinavian accent. The other characters in the film act like zombies, giving no reactions. Nevertheless, the cinematography is beautiful (the setting looks to me more like Utah than Israel), and there are some fine scenes. Stocked in many video chains.

*King of Kings I:* Cecil B. DeMille's production from 1927 is a movie classic. It was the first movie to use color: at the Resurrection, suddenly the black-and-white frames showing on-screen transformed into full color, dazzling audiences of the day. A relic of the silent era, the movie is a collective cliché of melodramatic facial expressions and violin soundtracks. It is safe for any group, however, and vastly entertaining; occasionally DeMille comes up with striking juxtapositions that shed new light on biblical texts. Available for purchase through some video chains and art film distributors or through Modern Sound Pictures in Omaha, Nebraska.

*King of Kings II:* Samuel Bronston remade DeMille's classic some thirty years later. Widely available, this movie stays mostly faithful to the gospel narratives, at least as seen through the eyes of Hollywood screenwriters.

*The Gospel According to St. Matthew:* I describe the impact of this movie in chapter 1 of *The Jesus I Never Knew.* Pasolini uses only the words of Matthew in presenting a unique portrayal of Jesus. Somewhat dated, the film has become a kind of period piece as well as an art film classic and is available through some of the art film distributors (Produced by Vanguard Video). Safe for any group.

*Witnesses:* Curt Cloninger, a fine actor who often performs at Youth Specialties conventions, has produced an entertaining video that gives glimpses of Jesus as seen by some of his contemporaries: the innkeeper, Zirim; the tailor, Abe; Lazarus; the demoniac; Barabbas; Thomas; and Peter. This film is ideal for groups, because it is already divided into short vignettes, each of which would make a provocative opening for a small group meeting. Available through Gospel Films. Curt also has a more recent video, *Red Letter Edition . . . Jesus Talks,* which presents vignettes from Jesus' life in a contemporary context.

*The Gospel Road:* Johnny Cash made this film as a labor of love, starring himself and his wife, June Carter Cash. The acting is stiff, the presentation schmaltzy. But if you like country-and-western music, you'll find some enjoyment here. May still be available through Christian film distributors or through the producer, World Wide Publications (based in Minneapolis).

*The Last Temptation of Christ:* Perhaps I should not even mention this film, since its release sparked furious controversy and a nationwide boycott. Some churches may find it so offensive as to have nothing to do with it. Indeed, the movie contains objectionable scenes as well as speculative and perhaps heretical theology (especially in the last forty minutes of the film). Yet I must admit that individual scenes scattered here and there throughout the film have great power. Taken as a whole, the film is a bore, hardly deserving the intense reactions it aroused. Taken in pieces, it offers much food for thought. It is available for rental in local video stores, and a wise leader can, with discretion, incorporate some scenes into a group discussion. Everything depends on the group.

If some members are easily offended or have a visceral reaction against the very idea of using this movie, don't force it. Note that Paul Schroeder, who wrote the screenplay, attended Calvin College, although he later abandoned much of his faith.

*Cotton Patch Gospel:* Another movie to use with discretion. Clarence Jordan, a radical Christian who founded the Koinonia commune in KKK territory in Georgia during the 1960s, paraphrased some of the New Testament into a hip, highly politicized version. Later Harry Chapin wrote musical accompaniment, and the *The Cotton Patch Gospel of Matthew* went on a road show. In this video, the actor Tom Key combines with a bluegrass band to present a version of Jesus' life set in places like Atlanta and Nashville rather than Jerusalem and Nazareth. Some Christians find the entire notion offensive. Others find it a delightful, refreshing portrayal. Most everyone agrees that the music is winsome in places. Should be available from Christian film distributors (produced by Bridgestone Productions).

*Godspell:* To my knowledge, this movie is no longer available for sale, although sometimes it is shown on HBO or other pay channels. If a group member notices a showing (movies about Jesus usually get airplay around Christmas and Easter), the group may want to devote an entire meeting to watching it together. It's funky, overwrought, and dated, showing the excesses of the sixties at their worst. At the time of release, however, it helped change the consciousness of many people, giving them a new vision of Jesus as a clown dressed up in a Superman outfit. Despite the weird settings, the musical's texts tend to stay faithful to the Gospels.

*Heaven:* This bizarre film by Diane Keaton is a documentary on how people view God, heaven, and the afterlife. Occasionally it borders on parody, but a few choice two- to three-minute segments are sure to draw laughs while at the same time raising important issues. The film also gives a disturbing picture of how Christians sometimes come across to others. Can be rented or purchased through some major video chains.

*Jesus of Montreal:* Must be used with discretion, as it contains some nudity and clearly unorthodox theology. Yet the movie is one of the most creative attempts in recent years to bring Jesus into a modern context. An acting troupe in Montreal takes on the task of presenting the Passion play in new forms, and in the process the actor playing Jesus becomes obsessed, even delusional, acting out new variations on scenes from Jesus' life. Provocative and powerful when viewed as a whole, the movie would probably work best in individual scenes when used in a group, since some of the content might be offensive. Can be purchased or rented through the major video chains.

*Jesus Christ, Superstar:* Hollywood made an arty version of the Broadway musical. It's all spectacle and fluff, and I never found much usable material in it, but it does present some arty scenes with a strong musical background.

Others: Don't limit yourself to full-length movies about Jesus. You can easily adapt individual scenes from, say, *Oh, God!* starring George Burns and John Denver, or from the more recent *Dear God* or from the TV show *Touched by an Angel* or from the rash of movies about angels. Use your creativity. If one of your favorite movies includes a scene of supernatural mystery or of prayer or portrays a Christian in a certain light, it may well prompt a good discussion on the topic.

If you want further background on the movies, a book titled *Divine Images: A History of Jesus on the Screen,* by Roy Kinnard and Tim Davis, gives extensive coverage of just about every movie ever made about Jesus.